1975

Motive and Method

in The Cantos of Ezra Pound

Edited by LEWIS LEARY

COLUMBIA UNIVERSITY PRESS

NEW YORK AND LONDON

Contents

Editor's Note

The first two of the essays here printed were read at the 1953 meeting of the English Institute at Columbia University. The second two are added because each develops an approach toward better understanding of the most difficult and most rewarding poem of our century: Sister Bernetta underlines the "Metamorphosis from Ovid" and Mr. Read the "descent into Hades from Homer"—the two themes on which Mr. Pound once told William Butler Yeats *The Cantos* was built. Unless otherwise indicated, quotations are from the New Directions edition of *The Cantos* and of other writings of Mr. Pound, and D. D. Paige's *The Letters of Ezra Pound*.

Though this volume is small, many have contributed to it: Mr. Pound by friendly suggestions which, if they could all have been followed, would have made it a better book; Norman Holmes Pearson by introducing the editor to Mr. Read; Clark Emery by allowing editorial use of portions of his unpublished study of Mr. Pound; Wilbur Frohock by providing at the English Institute an excellently provocative introduction to *The Cantos;* and Achilles Fang by a paper read at the Institute which served admirably as prelude to the first public playing of Mr. Pound's recordings of certain of his poems.

Motive and Method

in The Cantos of Ezra Pound

The Broken Mirrors and the Mirror of Memory

The title of the 1909 *Personae,* Pound's earliest collection of verse to achieve general circulation, implies not merely masks but a man donning them. It is the first of a long sequence of efforts on his part to draw our attention to the status of the poetic process itself as the central drama of his poetry. He will not have us think of him as a medium in which things happen, nor yet as a poet-hero striding and declaiming before backdrops of his own design. He will not, in fact, have us think of him at all: but he will ensure our awareness of his existence, exploring, voyaging, selecting, gathering experiences into a mind in which toward the close of his magnum opus they remain like Wagadu's City, "indestructible." The operations of this mind afford the dramatic continuity of *The Cantos;* but we do not always hear the unmistakably personal tone by which it announces its presence. As a personality, it makes strategic entrances and withdrawals. As a poetic agent, it is never absent for an instant. At the beginning of the poem the personality is in abeyance. Our attention is focused on Odysseus. We are not aware that a modern poet is telling the story: this Odysseus remains Homer's.

This commerce of the old and the new slips into the scheme of the poem with an unobtrusiveness so precise that a new reader is unlikely for some time to grasp its thematic weight. We have grown accustomed to watching the modern poet in the act of wresting his materials out of their own contexts into the dramatic contexts he provides for them, and when we see that happening— for example, in *The Waste Land*—we feel assured that the man is properly about his business, and attend with vigilance. Pound's way, however, is to await with a vigilance of his own the exact events that will enter his purposes without modification; the result is an undisturbed surface which, as Eliot remarked of Ben Jonson's, "reflects only the lazy reader's fatuity." Hence the appearance Canto I presents of a brilliant paraphrase of some lines of Homer's, with a few enigmatic phrases tacked on at the end: a bit of Homer pasted onto the title page of Pound's album, to preface the bits of Ovid, Cavalcanti, Sordello, Sappho, Confucius, and Lincoln Steffens.

This effect is the liability of a carefully calculated risk. Pound is determined to dispel at the start the notion that the things in his poem are symbols: that he says what he seems to be saying only as a way of saying something else. Canto I is not an elaborate metaphor. Nevertheless it is not "just Homer." Such a phrase, for one thing, is impertinent. Homer is not just a Greek document, he contains, incarnates, a paideuma. And the Canto, informed by that paideuma, *does* a great deal more than at first glance it *is,* and ultimately is what it does—something surprisingly comprehensive. Among other functions, it is one half of a parable for the complete Poundian doctrine of the creative act (Canto II is the other half).

In Canto I we have ritual, magic, homage to forerunners, and ghosts supplied with blood which enables them to speak in the present. The journey to the homes of the dead must be the first enterprise of the artist in quest of what is called in *Hugh Selwyn Mauberley* "his true Penelope." Piety to his forerunners is an element in this journey. The Elpenor who fell off Circe's ladder after a night of "abundant wine" reminds us of

> how Johnson (Lionel) died
> By falling from a high stool in a pub

and it is a pleasant coincidence that Odysseus' stele for his lost crewman ("A man of no fortune and with a name to come") has its parallel in Pound's preface to his selection of Lionel Johnson's poems. The blood for the ghosts is an analogue for translation; he brings them blood, and they speak anew with their own voices. Appropriately, translation is the mode of this Canto; with the aid of a Renaissance crib, Homer's Greek acquires the blood of Pound's English. It is not only the oldest surviving poetry in the Greek language, it is also, Pound thinks, the oldest part of Homer's subject matter: "The Nekuia shouts aloud that it is *older* than the rest ... hintertime ... *not* Praxiteles, not Athens of Pericles, but Odysseus" (*Letters,* p. 274). So it goes into the oldest available English, the rhythms and locutions of the Anglo-Saxon *Seafarer*. The whole makes a great piece of twentieth-century verse; and at the end of it the vision of a goddess is vouchsafed:

> Venerandam,
> In the Cretan's phrase, with the golden crown, Aphrodite.

She is the archetype of what comes out of the flux, and she manifests herself briefly to reward these labors.

Pound is always aware in this way of a drama implicit in the very application of words to things. In Canto XXIII we find him at work translating a bit of Greek—

> With the sun in a golden cup
> and going toward the low fords of ocean

—in the company of scientists not spinning abstractions but working toward useful results, Gemisto preferring explicit political actions to a dispute about the procession of the Holy Ghost, and Psellos declaring that the intellect is God's fire, omniform. This Canto, like the first, ends with the birth of Aphrodite:

> and saw then, as of waves taking form,
> As the sea, hard, a glitter of crystal,
> And the waves rising but formed, holding their form.
> No light reaching through them.

Something formed and permanent emerges from the flux of experience; this is a conquest over chaos requiring a technique as exact as M. Curie's scientific training.

Of the three long poems Pound wrote before embarking on *The Cantos,* the earliest, "Near Perigord" (1915), while it is the least impressive, most repays exegetical investigation. It is an elaborate parable of the poetic enterprise.

Bertrans de Born, one of Pound's first personae, wrote, as everyone knows, a canzone assembling the perfections of seven Provençal beauties to make an "ideal lady" in lieu of one named Maent who had turned him out. The task Pound sets himself in "Near Perigord" is to educe from documentary fragments a satisfying image of Bertrans, his selfhood and his world, so as to answer the question whether the poem is what it seems to be, an expression of thwarted love, or whether it is a political maneuver designed to flatter the seven beauties, set their lords at strife with Maent's lord whose castle menaced his line of communications, and win his jongleur a spy's access to their strongholds. There is nothing for Pound to work with but chance facts, and facts are suggestive but impenetrable: anecdotes about Bertrans' character, observations on the layout of the terrain, precedents for singing love when you mean war. The first part of the poem canvasses the facts and ends where it began:

> What is Sir Bertrans' singing?
> Maent, Maent, and yet again Maent,
> Or war and broken heaumes and politics?

In the second part we "try fiction"; three or four scenes visualized in the mind's eye, hypothetical visions groping toward the living truth:

> Let us say we see
> En Bertrans, a tower room at Hautefort,
> Sunset, the ribbon-like road lies, in red cross-light,
> Southward toward Montaignac, and he bends at a table
> Scribbling, swearing between his teeth; by his left hand
> Lie little strips of parchment covered over,
> Scratched and erased with *al* and *ochaisos*.
> Testing his list of rhymes, a lean man? Bilious?
> With a red straggling beard?
> And the green cat's eye lifts toward Montaignac.

This is plausible enough, and it is also an achievement in vivid re-creation, but we do not know if it is what a visitor would have seen, circa 1190. Nor would a contemporary's testimony necessarily have been helpful. The section ends with a pair of contemporaries, Arnaut Daniel and Richard Plantagenet, discussing the problem after Bertrans' death:

"You knew the man."

"*You* knew the man."

"I am an artist, you have tried both métiers."

"You were born near him."

"Do we know our friends?"

"Say that he saw the castles, say that he loved Maent!"

"Say that he loved her, does it solve the riddle?"

Those who "knew" him were as baffled as we who know only documents. The image of Bertrans is still eluding us. Suddenly, out of this chaos, Dante Alighieri educes a form:

Surely I saw, and still before my eyes
Goes on that headless trunk, that bears for light
Its own head swinging, gripped by the dead hair,
And like a swinging lamp that says, "Ah me!
I severed men, my head and heart
Ye see here severed, my life's counterpart."

This, not anything recoverable from documents or from the testimony of any acquaintance however intimate, is the image of Bertrans de Born that has persisted for six hundred years. It does not directly assist our present enquiries, but it is unchallengeably real. The one reality that no discussion shakes is evinced by art.

The living Bertrans perplexed his contemporaries; what we can learn of him perplexes us. Fact is grist for guesses. But no commentary can bring further light to what Dante has done in these lines, and no inquisition embarrass it.

The introduction of this pasage from Dante suddenly catalyzes the poem Pound is writing; into the anxious climate of research into enigmatic life it brings the cool steady air of Art, and incites the recollection that Bertrans' canzone was a work of art, before it occurred to anyone to treat it as a document. Since it is a work of art, its focus is on its subject Maent, and the final portion of Pound's poem moves swiftly to an image of Maent herself:

> She who could never live save through one person,
> She would could never speak save to one person,
> And all the rest of her a shifting change,
> A broken bundle of mirrors . . . !

Bertrans' canzone, in other words, is literally accurate homage: Maent herself, like the lady in the canzone, *was* a collection of fragments. Perhaps it was a love-poem. Perhaps it sang of war. Perhaps it had this or that personal motivation. But preeminently, it was imitation in the Aristotelian sense: an arrangement of words and images corresponding to the mode of being possessed by the subject. Our researches via fact and fiction were inconclusive because we were looking at the poet and not at what he was writing about: a woman not yet "awakened," with brilliant surfaces but no center. Pound imagines her response to Bertrans' declaration of love:

> "Why do you love me? Will you always love me?
> But I am like the grass, I cannot love you."

Or "Love, and I love, and love you,
And hate your mind, not *you,* your soul, your hands."

"Like the grass," having no personal center from which to direct
her affections; or "I love, and love you, / And hate your mind,"
loving therefore like a Provençal Emma Bovary a shadowy Bertrans, not the man himself.

Bertrans' paradoxical triumph, that of an artist, was to bring
form out of such a flux; the form was not that of Aphrodite, but
that of a composite lady. It was—and is—the form of what was
there. Pound attempted something similar in his "Portrait d'une
Femme," an image of a lady whose mind is a Sargasso Sea:

and yet,
For all this sea-horde of deciduous things,
Strange woods half-sodden, and new brighter stuff:
In the slow float of differing light and deep,
No! there is nothing! In the whole and all,
Nothing that's quite your own.
Yet this is you.

This is the same sort of woman as Maent; she exists only as a sort
of nodal point in the flux, where "ideas, old gossip, oddments of
all things" have collected. Superficially, the poem has nothing
whatever in common with Bertrans' canzone: Maent is an accumu-
lation of feminine perfections, not a sort of junkshop. The woman
of Pound's poem, however, is the early twentieth-century London
incarnation of this persistent human type: the "broken bundle of
mirrors." She reflects fragments of the events around her, and her
appropriate imagery is that of the romantic deliquescence, amber-

gris, mandrakes, redolent curiosa, as different as possible from the Provençal crispness reflected by her predecessor Maent.

What Pound has done in the poem, and what he implies Bertrans did in the canzone, is define a person who incarnates the flux itself. To define something, to coerce the motions of the sea of experience into a form, is the first business of the artist. This is the meaning of Aphrodite's birth from the sea foam. It is also the business of the person, and some people manage to imprint themselves unmistakably on the events by which they are surrounded. Sigismundo Malatesta was one of these. It is because Malatesta and Pound have similar objectives that Pound has presented Malatesta, in Cantos VIII–XI, through the medium of the circumambient events themselves. The man's personality emerges as powerfully from the miscellany of documents in *The Cantos* as it emerged from the welter of events chronicled by the documents. This is imitation once more; Malatesta has the same sort of intelligible existence in the poem that he had in fact.

This recalls us to Canto II, the theme of which is form out of flux. By form is meant intelligible form, like Aphrodite visible to the mind's eye. This Canto has, to be sure, a good deal to do with metamorphosis as well as with the sea; but the point about metamorphosis is that it implies a change of matter, not really of form. The swimming nymph transformed into a growth of coral is still the same person, rigid, brittle, and uncompliant. Her intelligible form, if not the physical form which is merely a silhouette of matter, remains what it was. But in her new state we see more easily what she is. This Canto polarizes Canto I. If translation—recreation—is one lobe of the poetic act, the eduction of forms is the other. The two are not antithetical: Canto II contains a translated passage (from Ovid), and Canto I performs a metamorphosis—Greek to Latin to English.

Canto II opens with four cryptic lines which condense the themes canvassed in "Near Perigord":

> Hang it all, Robert Browning,
> there can be but the one "Sordello."

"Sordello" the poem, like Dante's image of Bertrans, is art and hence final, defying modification, despite the questions that still haunt the documents Browning worked from.

> But Sordello, and my Sordello?

But Sordello the living man, whose heart, despite the finality of Browning's poem, remains for us strangers a dark forest? And Pound's Sordello—the image of the living man that forms in Pound's mind and is not identical with the one that formed in Browning's?

> Lo Sordels si fo di Mantovana

This is a nugget of documentary fact. It is part of the documentary chaos Browning sloughed off in educing his hero. But it also typifies the sort of irreducible testimony Pound in pursuit of his own objectives is determined not to slough off; the sort of thing through which, rather than in spite of which, Pound is to present his own Renaissance hero, Sigismundo. People are not animated formulae: they exist amid a process which they mirror even in contending with it. Maent who was a broken bundle of mirrors, incarnate flux, is the extreme case of what every human being manifests. A man cannot be separated from his acts, nor acts from context, nor either from the traces they have left in document and oral tradition. These latter—the historian's "sources"—are in their very discreteness analogues of what they attest to. Browning was not occupied as Pound is with historical truth; for instance he altered—Pound says "with perfect right" [1]—the ending of Sordello's story to suit his own purpose. His way of making historical men and women real was not unlike that of Walter Scott—his imagination, spurred by historians' hints which he disregarded when they proved inconvenient or intractable, conceived dramatic characters, more or less in the image of Robert Browning, which were then projected onto a colorfully drawn background. The kind of "truth" Browning can claim is dramatic and psychological. Pound however wants his poem about history to be historically true—that is, an image of how things really happen, presented in terms of what happens in Pound's mind when he considers the records. Hence his distrust of Browning's or the school-of-Macaulay historians' kind of abstraction from fact. Things that really happened are also more interesting and complex than anything he can imagine. So his poetic achievement—his Aphrodite—is not to be a swimmer stepping out of the ocean but a crystallization into form of the flux itself.

Hence the details of Canto II. The fifth line is "So-shu churned in the sea." Whether So-shu was the Emperor San-so who made roads, as Pound in another place states, or a sky-god, or, as Achilles Fang has suggested, a misnomer for the poet also known as Li Po, does not matter: the point is that churning solidifies liquid. The entire Canto is concerned with the sea, Aphrodite's native element. It is the blue-gray liquid in which seals disport and snipe bathe;

[1] *Pavannes, and Divisions* (New York, 1918), p. 171.

but the right kind of eyes bent upon its depths are rewarded with anthropomorphic glimpses, the sea-god's "Lithe sinews of water," or "The smooth brows, seen, and half seen." Hence the sequence of images near the end of the Canto; in alternate lines the empiric flux and the form it conceals:

> Lithe turning of water,
>> sinews of Poseidon,
> Black azure and hyaline,
>> glass wave over Tyro,
> Close cover, unstillness,
>> bright welter of wave-cords

The key to Pound's method throughout *The Cantos* is his conviction that the things the poet sees in the sea of events are really there. They are not "creations" of his. Similarly, the values registered in the poem are not imported and affirmed by the poet, but discerned by him in the record of human experience. They are literally *there* to be discovered; it is not a twentieth-century poet-moralist, nor a consciousness colored by the shards of American Christianity, that puts them there. They are not even values created by Confucius or Erigena or Malatesta or anyone else. Their origin is not human, but divine. In the words of a formulation that comes very late in the poem,

> it is not man
> Made courage, or made order, or made grace.

This brings us to the gods, who are the archetypal forms. "A god," Pound wrote thirty-five years ago, "is an eternal state of mind"; he is manifest "when the states of mind take form." This sounds as though the gods were human creations; but Pound warns us in *Pavannes* that the word "eternal" is to be taken literally:

> Are all eternal states of mind gods?
> We consider them so to be.
> Are all durable states of mind gods?
> They are not.   (p. 23)

Anything originally human is at best merely durable; the eternal state of mind has an eternal object. One thing that fitted the poets of the nineties to be crewmen of Pound-Odysseus was their conviction that certain supernatural types recurred. The great postulate, in fact the great cliché, of their poetry is the permanence of hypostatized Beauty, the cruel mistress of the artist. Pound opens his anthology *Profile* with Arthur Symons's "Modern Beauty":

> I am Yseult and Helen, I have seen
> Troy burn, and the most loving knight lie dead.
> The world has been my mirror, time has been
> My breath upon the glass

This goddess, like her polar opposite, the woman who is a broken bundle of mirrors, has her characteristic incarnation in every great period of art. Whenever she turns up in Pound's poetry we can identify her by her eyes. In the fourteenth century she is the "Merciles Beauté" to whom Chaucer wrote,

> Your eyen two wol sleye me sodenly
> I may the beauté of hem nat susteyne   (Canto LXXXI)

In the fifteenth century she is the Venus of Jacopo del Sellaio, of whom Pound writes in an early poem, "The Picture":

> The eyes of this dead lady speak to me.
>
> (*Personae*, p. 73)

In the nineteenth century, when the arts themselves partake of a tepid and uncertain vitality, she is the woman in *Hugh Selwyn Mauberley* with the "yeux glauques" and the "half-ruin'd face" who sat for Rossetti and Burne-Jones:

> The Burne-Jones cartons
> Have preserved her eyes
>
> Thin, like brook-water,
> With a vacant gaze
>
> Questing and passive   (*Personae*, p. 192)

In 1945 she is a barefoot girl, "la scalza," who says "Io son' la luna" —I am the moon.

> la scalza   :   Io son' la luna
> and they have broken my house [2]   (Canto LXXXVI)

This new incarnation of the eternal Beauty is identified with Jacopo's vision and Arthur Symons's ruinous supernatural mistress near the end of Canto LXXX, where the moon-girl [3] rides

> with the veil of faint cloud before her
> Κύθηρα δεινὰ as a leaf borne in the current
> pale eyes as if without fire

[2] For other allusions, see *The Pisan Cantos*, pp. 16, 21, 30, 31, and 78.

[3] This is the barefooted moon-girl transfigured. "La scalza" is Cythera (Aphrodite) incarnate in Pisa, as the "pastorella dei suini" (*The Pisan Cantos*, pp. 38, 118) is Circe.

and in the next Canto finally brings "new subtlety of eyes" into the Pisan tent.

The continually reincarnated goddess is herself the supreme form won out of flux; but Pound goes beyond the nineties in not being content with doing her elegiac homage. The point of adducing her here is to illustrate Pound's belief in her actual existence. If the word "belief" makes for epistemological embarrassment, it can be qualified with quotation marks; at any rate, a faith that the flux contains intelligible forms not simply projected there by the observer underlies the whole enterprise of *The Cantos*. The details of the poem, as we began by remarking, look so casual because Pound is determined not to intensify them by the pressure of superimposed meanings; his objective, in which he succeeds often enough to make the work cohere, is to find the scenes, persons, incidents, and quotations that will release into the poem without coercion the meanings they intrinsically contain. What he is writing about is, finally, human intelligence and the direction of the human will amid the events of history. The difficulty is that as the pressure cannot be separated from the water, so these forces can be perceived and discussed only in terms of the events they combat or animate. Only artists incarnate their intelligence and will in works that live on after them, and while artists are "the antennae of the race," the means of the good life are won for most men by rulers whose work dies when the tradition of their personal intelligence has left it. Pound's analogy in *Jefferson and/or Mussolini* between the statesman and the artist is well known. Both are known through their works. But the artist's works are indisputably *there;* the statesman's, being cut in the unstable material of events themselves, need to be elucidated with a careful eye to the author's character and intention. Bertrans de Born, we can now see, was both artist and man of action, and in one instance operated in both métiers with a single work. Pound closed the inquiry in "Near Perigord" by considering the canzone as a work of art and so an image of its subject; this does not really answer the question about Bertrans' ulterior intentions at all, since there is no reason why a poem could not be a self-contained work of art and also an instrument of policy. It is not the final insight of "Near Perigord" but the whole poem itself that disposes of that question. Pound sees no reason for supposing that aesthetic completeness cuts a work off from action.

We can now see why Pound refuses to simplify parts of *The Cantos* by explaining in separate paragraphs who the people are, and what the situations are, before presenting the details in concrete terms. A character sketch of Sigismundo Malatesta would not be Sigismundo but a few epithets of the compiler's; an account of who is fighting whom and why would import an illusory clarity which the events simply do not possess. Furthermore, the provision of such cribs would relegate the concrete detail to the status of local color, whereas the whole meaning of the poem consists in Pound's insistence that such details are not the applied color but the reality itself in which the will and intelligence of Malatesta are to be discerned like the iron filings that reveal the contours of the magnetic field.

Writing of Jefferson, Pound has pointed out a parallel between the statesman's opportunism and "the opportunism of the artist, who has a definite aim, and creates out of the materials present. The greater the artist the more permanent his creation. And this is a matter of WILL." The tactics of the artist and the man of action are sufficiently alike to elucidate as well as contaminate each other. Both of them desire to bring a welter of accidental happenings into a current directed by the will, which will, in turn, is focused on patterns of order not enacted by fiat but perceived by the mind's eye. "Points," Pound has noted in the Preface to his translation of the Confucian *Analects,* "define a periphery"; as by two or three juxtaposed images one grasps a poet's intention, so in a few selected deeds and events one perceives the direction of will and degree of enlightenment attained by a man of affairs.

The distressing fact that action, however noble or successful, is enacted in transient materials—mere events—not only creates a difficulty for the author of *The Cantos* but impinges on the fundamental human appetite for permanence. In the first thirty Cantos there is a continual stress on devouring time and the strategies by which divers people have sought to transfer the immutability of art into fact. Sigismundo's immersion in a whirl of events which must often have seemed pointless is polarized by the interest he maintained throughout his campaigns in the progress of his work of art—the Tempio. His post bag, seized by the Sienese in the Pitigliano affair, contained letters from the architect about the design of the nave, bills for materials, remarks about "the silver for the small medal" (Sigismundo's thoroughness extended to the minutest details), and a long letter from his secretary about the misfortunes of the second load of Veronese marble. Pound eulogizes the completed Tempio in a few quiet phrases; the emphasis in the last Malatesta Canto is on the spoliation of Sigismundo's worldly fortunes: Fano, San Martino, Sogliano, Torrano,

. . . and the villa at Rufiano
Right up to the door-yard
And anything else the Rev^{mo} Monsignore could remember.
And the water-rights on the Savio.
(And the salt heaps with the reed mats on them
       Gone long ago to the Venetians)
And when lame Novvy died, they got even Cesena.

                            (Canto xi)

In Canto iii Ruy Diaz is presented in defeat,

With no hawks left there on their perches,
And no clothes there in the presses

In Canto iv Troy is down. In Canto vii the shade of Henry James broods over a ghostly Paris. In Canto xx Roland breaks his horn. It belongs to the nature of events that their flow sweeps men and cities away. Hence the recurrent images of men whose business lies amid events trying to make something permanent out of life. Ignez da Castro is murdered at the end of Canto iii; in Canto xxx her husband sets her corpse on the throne and bids the Lords of Lisbon do homage to her. In Canto xx the lotus-eaters, borne toward the cataract, contemplate their suave nails and their curling opium smoke and murmur amid their illusory permanence,

      "Feared neither death nor pain for this beauty;
If harm, harm to ourselves."

In Canto xvii the vanished Greek landscape of vines, clear water, and goddesses is reproduced by the Venetians in a "forest of marble." That the Venice Cantos—like Venice itself—possess great beauty no one denies. There is a limitation inherent in static beauty of this sort, however, which also inheres in the tone of the relevant passages. The city is full of "effects"—

> "marble leaf, over leaf,
> "silver, steel over steel,
> "silver beaks rising and crossing,
>
> . . . .
>
> Dye-pots in the torch-light,
> The flash of wave under prows

—but the effects terminate in themselves. Nothing happens except the play of light and darkness. Darkness in fact is the indispensable setting:

> "In the gloom the gold
> Gathers the light about it."

The gold needs the gloom. It is a lordly and sinister symbol. As in the stone forest, art by defying living process comes close to being a perversion of nature; so attempts to make gold breed, instead of relating its increased supply to the natural increment of grass and sheep, are the archetypal crime, usura: a crime at which the Venetians were very adept. Hence the human actions that occur in Venice partake of the deadliness of their setting and pervert or ignore its splendor: the Venetians betray their employee Carmagnola and execute him between two of their columns; a doge's wife will touch food only with golden forks, "Bringing in, thus, the vice of luxuria" (Canto XXVI).

All these attempts to educe stability from the flux, setting up a dead queen, fabricating a stone forest, are against nature, "contra naturam" (Canto xlv). They apotheosize the arrest of living processes. The sea in *The Cantos* is not only the image of flux but the source of life, as for Gemisto, who "stemmed all from Neptune" (Canto lxxxiii), it was the source of the gods. The archetype of these assaults on nature is the metamorphosis in Canto ii: seamen who defied the god are transformed into fish, and their swift ship into an immobile rock. Both permanence and movement are still present, but the thing which should move moves no more, and the men who should evince human stability are condemned to nose mindlessly through the flux. This is the obverse of the creative metamorphosis. In the same way that Venice rises out of the water the lotus-eaters float on its current, but the flow of events does not enter into their composition. They are part of Pound's *Inferno*, not his *Paradiso*. They partake of the separation of wealth from living processes for which his synecdoche is usura.

The great paradox of the poem, and one of its structural keys, is, then, that the conventionally splendid passages in the first third of the work deal with dead material. These passages achieve immediate acceptance from most readers because they are written according to romantic norms; but a discernible component in the sensibility to which they appeal is a lush acceptance of easeful death. The themes that Pound finds exciting, on the other hand, are presented in terms of minutely noted events, none of them overwhelmingly impressive but all of them in sequence defining a current of volition. The Adams Cantos in particular are explicitly devoid of lyrical appeal, their subject being the reverse of static. Their method is an expansion of that by which Sigismundo was characterized: dozens upon dozens of phrases are transcribed from Pound's sources—chiefly John Adams's own voluminous works—with as little modification as possible.

If it were only the nature of the will working among these events that interested Pound, the Adams Cantos could be briefer and more readily assimilable: Sigismundo was thoroughly presented in twenty-four pages. Adams requires eighty because Pound is equally interested in the nature of the events themselves: events like the writs of assistance, Adams's researches into the nature of government, or his negotiations with the French concerning the fisheries. This double focus—on Adams and on the specific things Adams was doing—deserves our explicit attention. One of the forces in the logic of the poem is brought to culmination in these Cantos. The eighty Adams pages are part of a poem and so are bounded, defined, interwoven, and self-consistent: they are not a random bushel of documents. On the other hand, they do not impose simplifying images on the events they deal with; their texture is the texture of those events. Adams remains a man in action, and his actions preserve their nature; Adams is not transformed into a sculptured hero in a static but indicative posture. From this midpoint we can see how everything in the earlier Cantos belongs in some sense to the past, and consents to lie down on the page because time has encased it. Even the Malatesta Cantos are somewhat elegiac. The Adams Cantos alone focus on the actual process of events. As the first two parts of "Near Perigord" concern themselves successively with "fact" and "fiction," so the first two thirds of the Cantos work in terms of fiction and fact. The method of Cantos i–xxx is preponderantly the re-creation of scene after scene; that of xxxi–lxxi the transcription of fact after fact.

If Adams was not "a broken bundle of mirrors," however, the Adams Cantos certainly are. The enterprise of the poem reaches in these pages an extreme tension: events, we agree, are intelligible, possess an actual, inherent intelligibility; but if we impose a concretizing image we kill process, doing in artifact what the Venetians did in fact, and if we adhere to the structure of events we lose a center and operate in terms of fragments. Neither of these extremes perhaps occurs in the poem, but everything in the poem up to the end of the Adams sequence can be located somewhere between their contrary tensions. How the form is to be seen and revealed in the flux without dissipation or misleading abstraction—however poetic the abstraction—is the problem for which, if the poem is to be successful, the final Cantos must present a satisfactory solution.

The Pisan Cantos—all that is so far available of the final third of the poem—do indeed attempt such a synthesis. There seems to be general agreement that they cohere in certain obvious ways not manifested by the Adams sequence. This does not mean that the Adams Cantos fail: the discreteness of their materials is part of the meaning of the poem; events when they are actually going on look like that; they come to the attention in sharp fragments and episodes, seriatim. Men when they are actually before us make themselves known in that way: a gesture, a revealing bit of speech, shards of obiter dicta. From such glimpses we acquire like archaeologists our knowledge of the civilization that is contemporaneous with us. Hence the vital relevance of Frobenius's methods. The materials in the Pisan Cantos are a great deal more heterogeneous than those of the Adams sequence, and most of the fragments are a great deal smaller: a word, a line, a glimpsed image. What holds

the events of the Pisan sequence together is that they are trans-
acted explicitly within Pound's mind. He brought with him European culture into the barbarians' stockade, and in his mind that
culture's past and the present exist side by side, a paideuma, to
their mutual elucidation. For the broken mirrors have been substituted what Pound calls in Canto xxxvii, in connection with
Martin Van Buren's *Autobiography,* "the mirror of memory."

Certain explicit links with the earliest sequence reinforce this
theme. In Canto xxx the episode of Ignez da Castro is introduced
with the phrase, "Time is the evil."

> Time is the evil. Evil.
>   A day, and a day
> Walked the young Pedro baffled,
>   a day and a day
> After Ignez was murdered.
> Came the Lords in Lisboa
>   a day, and a day
> In homage. Seated there
>   dead eyes,
> Dead hair under the crown,
> The King still young there beside her.

Time is the evil; Pedro's attempt to defy its ravages by setting
up her corpse beside him has its pathos as well as its valor. He is
"still young there beside her"; she will never get older, but neither
will she ever do anything again. In Canto lxxiv the phrase about
time recurs, but the spasmodic rhythm of the Ignez lines gives
way to an easy serenity in which all things are held in the memory
and time is denied:

> Time is not, Time is the evil, beloved
> Beloved the hours βροδοδάκτυλος
>> as against the half-light of the window
>> with the sea beyond making horizon
> le contre-jour the line of the cameo
> profile "to carve Achaia"
>> a dream passing over the face in the half-light

This particular memory fuses fact and artifact; it was a real person's profile, but a cameo besides. The cameo, the medallion, was the art at which Hugh Selwyn Mauberley labored,[4] but the one specimen of his work that we are shown encrusts the life of the subject, a singing woman, with analogies drawn from art books:

> The sleek head emerges
> From the gold-yellow frock
> As Anadyomene in the opening
> Pages of Reinach.   (*Personae,* p. 204)

This is precariously neat, but it paralyzes the woman of the poem at the same time as it turns Venus Anadyomene from a goddess into an art historian's illustration. As for Achaia, Pisanello (also in *Mauberley*) lacked the skill to imitate its style in medallions. Pound has drawn together in this passage from Canto LXXIV three unsuccessful attempts to defy the flux: King Pedro's, Mauberley's, and Pisanello's. They drop into place with an unforced casualness which itself effects a criticism of Mauberley's overdeliberate allusions. A random event—the remembered placing of a person's head against the window-light—achieves the victory over time and

---

[4] Mauberley's "Medallion" is meant to be contrasted with Pound's "Envoi" on the same subject (*Personae,* p. 197).

change which was denied to their willfulness or meticulousness.

The theme-word of Canto LXXXIII is "hudor"—water—the element of flux itself, now transformed into the element that brings life and peace:

> the sage
> delighteth in water
> the humane man has amity with the hills

On the third page of this Canto the stone trees of Venice growing out of the waters of the canal are counterpointed by the "hidden city" of living growth by a streamside:

> Δρυάς, your eyes are like the clouds over Taishan
> When some of the rain has fallen
> and half remains yet to fall

> The roots go down to the river's edge
> and the hidden city moves upward
> white ivory under the bark

At the end of Canto LXXIV the flux itself achieves form: through the mind courses a fountain whose "crystal jet," tossing its "bright ball," holds its sculptured form not in spite of the flow of water but because of it. The passage follows two pages of memories extending from Pound's childhood days in New York to the most recent events of his life in Europe. The flow of these reminiscences is transformed into that of the fountain:

> This liquid is certainly a
> property of the mind
> nec accidens est   but an element
> in the mind's make-up
> est agens and functions   dust to a fountain pan otherwise

These are among the key passages of the Pisan Cantos. All of them emphasize the primacy of the natural, of what is, over what the mind would prefer to impose. Their emphasis is on art as a product of will, but of will that has achieved the wisdom to adequate its processes to the nature of what is given.

This new emphasis on the natural does not undo the method of the earlier Cantos, but rather brings it to apotheosis. It is because the very first Canto accepted what was in Homer instead of *using* Homer, imbedding Homeric allusions into a narrative of Pound's, that in the last Cantos Pound can be so free with Homeric materials without violating the unity of his poem. Art will not happen of itself; it still requires an artist; but like Bertrans' canzone which seemed at first sight a fiat of synthesis, it embodies what the artist discovers in his material, not values he makes out of nothing. "Originality" consists in being able to *see* something, often to see that it has been done before. Hence the emphasis in the Pisan Cantos on the translators and re-creators who maintained a tradition by uncovering forgotten discoveries: Dolmetsch (whose very name means "interpreter"); Gavin Douglas; the young Pound who worked with Provençal and Chinese. This again has its precedent: in Canto xxviii we are told how Pound's grandfather, putting a railway through Wisconsin, coped with a shortage of rails by prying up track that had been abandoned in New York State and moving it to where it could be used. The old music laid up in archives was of no use to anyone till Dolmetsch happened along; nor were Homer's chthonic vigor or Propertius' elaborate wit active in the Anglo-Saxon consciousness until Ezra Pound recreated them.

Canto lxxv is a brief parable on creation and re-creation: like the Homer that passed through Greek, Latin, and Anglo-Saxon, Janequin's choral bird-music (the motifs of which, Pound has elsewhere suggested, are vastly older than Janequin) is transcribed for Francesco da Milano's Renaissance lute and Gerhart Münch's twentieth-century violin and piano; even in the violin part alone the birds are still audible. The piece nowhere mimics the songs of birds: it is imitation, something similar done in a different medium. The original feat of artifice was absolute, whether Janequin performed it or someone earlier than he. Once done, it can survive metamorphosis after metamorphosis. But it remains bird-music: it has some sort of sanction in the natural order.

These are the principles that control the endless variety of the Pisan Cantos. These Cantos elucidate the earlier Cantos by drawing our attention to the sort of truth that is aimed at throughout the poem: a revelation of events by honest presentation. The whole inheres in the details, so much so that the poem has come to be entitled with a word denoting the parts that enter its sum: not *Jerusalem Delivered* or *Paradise Lost* but simply *The Cantos*. And the parts do not disappear into the whole but maintain their individual qualities: indeed it is on their maintaining their individuality that the success of the whole depends. And the parts draw their individuality from the sources Pound actually used, the books he quotes, the scenes he recollects, with as little modification as possible. He is fanatical about facts and dates because the whole enterprise depends on leaving his materials as he finds them; this in turn depends on a faith in the inexhaustibility of the actual, and so in imitation—reflection—rather than fabrication. The "Hang it all, Robert Browning" of Canto II is ultimately generalized in the "Pull down thy vanity" of Canto LXXXI: the vanity there rebuked is the kind that supposes it can make a better order than it can discover.

This is the vanity of "proud man, dress'd in a little brief authority." The etymological sense of vanity—emptiness—takes us back to the thwarted makers of one of the early Cantos, whose lament, "Nothing we made, we set nothing in order," can be taken as literal truth. They set *nothing* in order. Nullity was their material. They were cutters in the stone pits, but instead of quarrying blocks for enduring building they erected "the vanity of Ferrara" (Canto xxv), where a council disputed as to "the which begat the what in the Trinity" (Canto xxvi). This pseudo culture—a counterfeit of the indestructible city of Dioce and Wagadu [5]—is the nothingness we are directed to "pull down."

The famous passage in Canto LXXXI is introduced with a hymn to the re-creators: Lawes and Jenkyns, who made both instruments and music, and Arnold Dolmetsch, who remade both three centuries later. Their music harmonizes with natural processes:

> Hast 'ou fashioned so airy a mood
> To draw up leaf from the root?
> Hast 'ou found   a cloud   so light
> As seemed neither mist nor shade?

Then, with a recollection of the intolerable eyes of Chaucer's Roundel, the unmistakable eyes of the eternal Aphrodite enter the poet's tent, "casting but shade beyond the other lights" and con-

[5] The city of Dioce (Canto LXXIV) reproduced on earth the pattern of the solar system (see Herodotus I. 96–99, also my note in the *Explicator*, December, 1952, item 20). The city of Wagadu was rebuilt four times and is "now in the mind indestructible" (Canto LXXIV); see Guy Davenport's "Pound and Frobenius" in this volume.

centrating in their brilliant dazzle the beauties of the natural order: sky's clear, night's sea, green of the mountain pool.

The next lines employ the image of refining gold: one applies intense heat, and skims off the refuse. The things in the mirror of memory have survived a long fire:

> What thou lovest well remains,
>
> > the rest is dross

Unlike the gold of Venice which implies a circumambient gloom, this gold of the mind cannot be stolen ("reft from thee"), it is both what you inherit and what you pass on ("thy true heritage"), and it eludes the possessive instinct ("Whose world, or mine or theirs / or is it of none?"). Then the fact that the artist must see before he can make is once more affirmed:

> First came the seen, then thus the palpable
> Elysium, though it were in the halls of hell

The lines against vanity are introduced by a final illustration of this principle: man need not pretend to make order, because every detail of the natural world proclaims it. "The ant's a centaur in his dragon world." The centaur, a Greek poet's invention, images the animal breaking into the rational. Like Bertrans' canzone it is not an irresponsible junction of disparities but an image of what actually exists: the natural condition of composite man. And in the insect kingdom there are corresponding hierarchies: among creatures that kill and cannibalize there exist the ants with their social organization. Hence:

> Pull down thy vanity, it is not man
> Made courage, or made order, or made grace

"Paquin," a few lines later, is a Parisian dressmaker; he typifies applied elegance, which not only draws out another sense of "vanity" but affords a contrast with the unforced beauty of an insect's functional "green casque."

The natural order even supplies analogues for human disorder. The dog ("Thou art a beaten dog beneath the hail") is a Rotarian beast who flatters our self-esteem because he needs our flattery of his own: ill-treatment takes all the starch out of him. The magpie ("A swollen magpie in a fitful sun") steals, and it also chatters in mimicry of what it doesn't understand. Against these deplorable emblems of human confusion is affirmed the validity of whatever portion of the life of the mind is occupied with the done rather than the not done, with the solid rather than the vain, with the social utility of gathering "from the air a live tradition" rather than the vanity of pursuing prestige and a reputation for cleverness.

When its materials are regarded in the mirror of memory, the poem resolves itself. The triumph that every reader has felt in the passage we have just been discussing is connected with Pound's satisfaction at not having attempted to force a premature resolution. He respected the idiosyncracies of his subject matter and it fused itself finally, because by long and ardent attention he was able to discover what Bertrans de Born discovered about the lady Maent: not the living principle it would have been fatally easy for the observer's mind to import, but the modes of coherence, always awaited but for most of the history of the acquaintance unguessed at, which in fact inhered.

Pound and Frobenius

> *Kung is modern in his interest in folk-lore.*
> *All this Frazer-Frobenius research is Confucian.*
>
> *Kulchur,* p. 272

Whether Ezra Pound has come upon a Confucian peace or whether the puma is still tense in his cage is hard to say: "At seventy," Master Kung told his pupils, "I could follow my heart's desire without overstepping the t-Square." [1] The *Odes,* which were to wait for translation until *The Cantos* was finished, are done; "Granpa in the bughouse" has turned to translating Sophocles,[2] and the *Paradiso* of the most controversial and difficult poem in the language is about to be begun. Canto C will probably not be the end. To learn both iconography and anatomy of the poem at this moment is a labor which must be accomplished without being able to see the total organism. "The poet looks forward to what is coming next in the poem," Pound has said concerning the completion of *The Cantos,* "not backward to what has been accomplished." [3] It was a warning against interpreting the Pisan group as a full recapitulation of the rest. This inquiry into certain

[1] *The Analects* II. 4 (Pound's translation).

[2] "Trachiniae." Asked if *The ABC of Reading* needed revision because of later considerations, Pound replied that he would give Sophocles the place Aeschylus now has in the text. Part of this conviction can be traced to F. R. Earp, whose criticism of Aeschylus and Sophocles has caused Pound to call him "the only man who knows anything about Greek."

[3] Interview at St. Elizabeth's Hospital, July 20, 1953.

passages in *The Cantos* is a partial attempt at clarifying both a direction of Pound's thought and a structural cohesion of images which seem to me vital to a conception of the poem's meaning so far.

As a postscript to *Guide to Kulchur* there is a list of books and documents such as Ezra Pound has been compiling for years, "found," as the editor notes, "among Mr. Pound's papers." The list is called a sextant, to be used presumably for that kind of Odyssean navigation which is a relentless theme of *The Cantos,* πολλῶν δ'ἀνθρώπων ἴδεν ἄστεα καὶ νόον ἔγνω—"many were the men whose cities he saw and whose mind he learned"—and contains everything the reader familiar with the enthusiasms and direction of *The Cantos* would expect to find: the Chinese classics, the *Odyssey,* Greek tragedy, Brooks Adams, the English Charters, Blackstone, and the Constitution. The fifth item in the list, however, is a new insight; not a surprise, certainly, but a part of Pound's learning singularly neglected by his critics and commentators. "Frobenius:" the fifth section of the sextant reads, "Erlebte Erdteile: [4] without which a man cannot place any book or work of art in relation to the rest." Were it not for the high incidence of Frobenius in Pound's correspondence, the vigorous formal appearance of Frobenius's influence in *Guide to Kulchur* (loudly and gratefully acknowledged), the notes on him in the six Money Pamphlets, and his vivid emergence in *The Cantos,* particularly the Pisan group, Pound's discovery of Frobenius and

[4] Leo Frobenius, *Erlebte Erdteile,* Ergebnisse eines deutschen Forscherlebens (Frankfurt am Main, 1929), 7 vols. (I. Ausfahrt: Von der Völkerkunde zum Kulturproblem; II. Erschlossene Räume: Das Problem Ozeanien; III. Vom Schreibtisch zum Äquator; IV. Paideuma: Umrisse einer Kultur- und Seelenlehre; V. Das sterbende Afrika; VI. Monumenta Africana; VII. Monumenta Terrarum).

the claim made for his wisdom in the sextant would be even more obscure than they are at present.

Pound believes, but cannot be certain, that Henri Gaudier-Brzeska may have mentioned Frobenius to him first, although it was 1925 or 1926 before he began reading him.[5] It was the first time that Pound had bothered to read a book in German since 1909.[6] William Butler Yeats wrote T. Sturge Moore in 1929:

> Ezra Pound has just been in. He says, "Spengler is a Wells who has founded himself on German scholarship instead of English journalism." He is sunk in Frobenius, Spengler's German source, and finds him a most interesting person. Frobenius suggested the idea that cultures (including arts and sciences) arise out of races, express those races as if they were fruit and leaves in a pre-ordained order and perish with them. . . . He proved from his logic—some German told Ezra— that a certain civilization must have existed at a certain spot in Africa and then went and dug it up. He proved his case all through by African research.[7]

Although the scope of this study does not allow for an analysis of *The Cantos,* it should be seen that in order to be concerned seriously with the nigh casual lines in which Frobenius appears as a character we must establish the poem as one which speaks history and theory along with its other functions. Its multiplicity of subjects and directions are controlled by a singleness of purpose which is a core of doctrine as rich in fused sensibilities as the structure of the poem itself.

[5] Letter, undated [March, 1953].
[6] Interview at St. Elizabeth's Hospital, July 19, 1953.
[7] Joseph Hone, *W. B. Yeats* (New York, 1943), p. 405.

For forty years [Pound says in *An Introduction to the Economic Nature of the United States*] I have schooled myself, not to write the Economic History of the U.S. or any other country, but to write an epic poem which begins "In the Dark Forest", crosses the Purgatory of human error, and ends in the light, *"fra i maestri di color che sanno."* For this reason I have had to understand the NATURE of error.

The method of "understanding error" which Pound chose led him to seek a center of reason which became his orthodoxy. In *Make It New* he took an almost religious stand in saying he believed the *Ta Hio*. He believes deeply in the efficacy of the Confucian sincerity, his translations of the *Ta Hio* (The Great Digest), *Chung Yung* (The Unwobbling Pivot), and *Lun Yü* (The Analects) showing a greater dexterity of conviction, probably, than any other of his translations. Pound's orthodoxy has a rigorous structure; our interest here is his claiming a place in that "unwobbling pivot" —Confucius' center of the compass—for the work of Leo Frobenius.

When *The Cantos* is finished and given a name, the title page will bear three emblems, the Chinese character for sincerity, 誠 and two prehistoric African rock figures of hunters, from drawings made by Frobenius in the Libyan desert.[8] Those who saw Frobenius at his exhibition of cave paintings at the Museum of Modern Art in 1938 can appreciate Pound's saying that "we looked as if we came from the same egg," an identification that sinks deeper than physiognomy when we look to *The Cantos,* especially behind the persona of Odysseus. There is a certain quality of af-

[8] Interview at St. Elizabeth's Hospital, July 20, 1953.

fection active wherever Frobenius comes on scene. The first time
we notice him he is practicing the ancient rite of rain making in
Baluba, and succeeding. In Canto xxxviii:

> The white man who made the tempest in Baluba
> Der im Baluba das Gewitter gemacht hat . . .
>> they spell words with a drum beat

which by Canto liii is set alongside the proper processes of agriculture and economics:

> so that in 1766 Tching Tang opened the copper mine (ante
>> Christum)
> made discs with square holes in their middles
>> and gave them to the people
> wherewith they might buy grain
>> where there was grain
>
> The silos were emptied
> 7 years of sterility
>> der im Baluba das Gewitter gemacht hat

Frobenius as rain maker can be traced further through *The Cantos;*
his fight to save West Africans from deportation to Australia is
nowhere mentioned. "It is the quality of thought in Frobenius,"
Pound says, "which is important." [9] Frobenius's subject matter

[9] Crediting Frobenius with first treating cultures as living organisms, José Ortega
y Gasset (*Las Atlantidas* [2d ed., Buenos Aires, 1943]) criticizes his accomplishment as follows: "Si Frobenius y Spengler no hubiesen abandonado la latitud del
puro empirismo histórico, que es donde sus ideas resultan fecundas y comproba-
bles, habrían realizado una labor ejemplar. Pero al darles una dimensión metafísica,
y, por tanto, absoluta, han quitado la razón a sus proprios pensamientos." But it

has had its influence on Pound, but first an analysis of his method
of work and inquiry should serve as an introduction to his importance in the core of orthodoxy.

Among the Money Pamphlets, *Carta da visita* (Rome, 1942)
gives most attention to Frobenius as a historian of urgent value.

> We find two forces in history: [Pound says in the second
> part of the pamphlet, "The State,"] one that divides, shatters,
> and kills, and one that contemplates the unity of the mystery.
> "The arrow hath not two points."
>
> There is the force that falsifies, the force that destroys every
> clearly delineated symbol, dragging man into a maze of ab-
> stract arguments, destroying not one but every religion.

Allowing for the more obvious rationale behind this statement,
Frobenius's study of Africa, after it had been destroyed as a tri-part
culture—Erythraean, Syrtic, and Atlantic [10]—by internal rot and
external exploitation, stands as Pound's ideal of historic method:

---

is exactly the *dimensión metafísica* in which Pound is interested: where Frobenius
moves his discussion from "cultures" to "culture"—"cultures at their *most*," as
Pound puts it.

Pound sees both Agassiz and Frobenius as developers of the work of Friedrich
Heinrich Alexander, Baron von Humboldt (1769–1859). *Vide* Humboldt and
Aimé Bonpland, *Voyage aux régions équinoxiales du nouveau continent*, 1807 (30
vols.), and Humboldt, *Kosmos*, 1845–62 (5 vols.).

[10] These are the cultures built up in Africa from without, having been absorbed
into the indigenous cultures which they enriched and transformed. "No people on
earth has its 'own' culture" (Frobenius), all cultural developments growing among
a people according to the richness of their "stored stimuli," their capacity for as-
similating new acquisitions, and their "gift of shaping such acquisitions into forms
in harmony with the style natural to the people concerned and then developing
them organically." For a concise statement of a part of Frobenius's work, see his
"Early African Culture as an Indication of Present Negro Potentialities," American
Academy of Political and Social Science, *Annals*, CXL (November, 1928), 153–65.

to see through the debris of a civilization its paideumic structure
which somehow is never lost and which is ripe for rejuvenation and
influence from the best of other cultures, provided the nature of
error which ruined it can be known and removed.

> I know you jib at China and Frobenius cause they aint pie
> church, [Pound wrote to T. S. Eliot in February of 1940] and
> neither of us likes sabages, black habits, etc. However, for yr.
> enlightenment, Frazer worked largely from documents. Frob.
> went to *things,* memories still in the spoken tradition, etc. His
> students had to *see* and be able to draw objects. All of which
> follows up Fabre *and* the Fenollosa "Essay on Written Char-
> acter."

And in the same letter:

> Naturally history without monetary intelligence is mere
> twaddle. That I think I have conveyed to you by now?? But I
> bayn't sure you have grosp the other element in the growth of
> historiographic *teXne.* I should use both that distance from
> *Nichomachean* notes to *Magna Moralia,* along with various
> categories of Frobenius.
>
> That I cd. start on now. I don't think I am ready for an
> analysis of Christianity into its various racial components,
> European and non-European. Think I should approach it in
> such a book—natr of belief, etc.
>
> Note that I shd. claim to get on from where Frobenius left
> off, in that his Morphology was applied to savages and my
> interest is in civilizations at their *most.*

The letter had begun:

There is, so far as I know, no English work on Kulturmorphologie, transformation of cultures. Can't use a German
term at this moment. Morphology of cultures. Historic process
taken in the larger (*Letters,* p. 336).

In the next section of *Carta da visita* the Frobenius intelligence
is claimed for Brooks Adams,

> who was, as far as I know, the first to formulate the idea of
> *Kulturmorphologie* in America. His cyclic vision of the West
> shows us a consecutive struggle against four great rackets,
> namely the exploitation of the fear of the unknown (black
> magic, etc.), the exploitation of violence, the exploitation or
> the monopolization of cultivable land, and the exploitation of
> money.

Frobenius's educated eye, its ability to see not only from which
culture a potsherd comes but also where in the culture it belongs,
Pound feels is a concomitant quality of enlightenment. "To have
gathered from the air a live tradition," the achievement at the
center of both men's work, is the measure of cultural level to be
studied whenever Pound exhibits Frobenius as teacher. Note this
emphasis in the introduction to *Confucio: studio integrale:* "*Ci
ha lasciato il testamento . . . una tradizione orale, venerata dai
discepoli . . .*" and in Canto LXXXI:

> What counts is the cultural level,
> > thank Benin for this table ex packing box
> > "doan yu tell no one I made it"
> > > from a mask fine as any in Frankfurt

Using the telling title "Kulturmorphologie" he adjusts Frobenius's insight to his statement of Canto XLV:

> Usura is a murrain, usura
> blunteth the needle in the maid's hand
> and stoppeth the spinner's cunning. Pietro Lombardo
> came not by usura
> Duccio came not by usura
> nor Pier della Francesca; Zuan Bellin' not by usura
> nor was 'La Calunnia' painted.
>
> . . . .
>
> Usura rusteth the chisel
> It rusteth the craft and the craftsman

But to see the corrosion of usury in architectural or painting style is a perception to be learned from Frobenius:

> To repeat: an expert, looking at a painting (by Memmi, Goya, or any other), should be able to determine the degree of the tolerance of usury in the society in which it was painted. . . . "The character of the man is revealed in every brush-stroke" (and this does not apply only to ideograms).[11]

[11] Considering Pound's passion for sextants and quadrants (he always uses the tag "Dichten-condensare" when on the subject of the morphology of cultures and the writing of text books), Frobenius's five proposals—one of many, like Pound's one-page guides to "all that a man needs to know"—to Adolf Bastian at the time of Rivière's discovery that the Altamira cave paintings in Spain, discovered in 1879 by Baron Sautoula, were done in the Ice Age, should be of interest:

1. The most difficult obstacle to our understanding of culture is our ignorance. We do not know enough. Any trained zoologist, given the leg of a beetle, can tell you the name of the bug it belongs to, and no botanist supposes that roses bloom on oak trees. We are familiar with the characteristics of the chemical elements, know how they are combined, and that in combination they again have different

Further notations on Frobenius in *Carta da visita* make clear
the extent to which Pound has assimilated him into the core of
his orthodoxy:

> The writings of Frobenius contain flashes of illumination.
> From nineteenth-century philology, relegating everything to
> separate compartments, creating specialists capable of writing
> monographs or articles for encyclopedias without the least
> understanding of their import or relation to the total problem,
> Frobenius advanced to Kulturmorphologie. He brought the
> living fact to bear on the study of dead documents. It began—
> *incipit vita nova sua*—with his hearing that certain railway
> contractors were in conflict with some local tradition. A king
> and a girl had driven into the ground where there was a cer-
> tain hillock: they ought not to make a cutting through that

characteristics. We even know what these characteristics are. But what do we know
about culture? Nothing. Because we are lazy, phlegmatic, and stupid, because we
plume ourselves if we can string together five or ten citations to write a witty,
anecdotal paper.

2. What do we need then? Work! And more work! Every fact, object, and
belief which can help us to understand the growth of human culture should be
recorded and indexed for use. It is a pure question of application, first to get the
material together and then to see how much we can learn alone from the geo-
graphic distribution of certain culture elements.

3. We will find that there are peoples of whom we do not know enough, and
so it will be necessary to send out expeditions to find and gather the material we
lack.

4. It will be our task to handle our material not only linguistically, descriptively,
and philologically but also graphically. That means that every expedition will be
equipped with a staff of artists who will transfer to paper and canvas that which
cannot be accurately recorded with a camera.

5. That is to say, one of the main tasks of a future serious "science of culture"
and of a true culture-morphology will be to establish institutions for research and
to send out expeditions.

Quoted in Leo Frobenius and Douglas C. Fox, *African Genesis* (Faber and
Faber, 1938).

sacred place. The materialist contractors took no notice and went ahead—and unearthed a bronze car with effigies of Dis and Persephone.

Later he wrote, "Where we found these rock drawings there was always water within six feet of the surface."

And again in *Carta da visita:*

> The modern university was founded at Frankfurt by Leo Frobenius, or, at least it was the first approach to the modern university. If I had been thirty-five years younger, I would have wanted to enroll myself as a student.

Frobenius's work, to my knowledge, has been recognized outside its own incredible obscurity at Frankfurt and in the field by three irreconcilable enterprises: Ezra Pound's enthusiasm; Dr. Carl Jung's use of his theories, mainly those concerning mythology; [12] and the work of Oswald Spengler, who regarded Frobenius as teacher and whose *Untergang des Abendlandes* is the most obvious and celebrated offshoot of Frobenius's work.[13] Anthropologists tend not to know who he is. That he has fructified the

---

[12] See Jung's *The Psychology of the Unconscious* and the introduction to Jung and Kerényi's *Essays on a Science of Mythology.*

[13] Spengler's statement of what he considered of most importance in Frobenius's work: "We will consider the first stage as that of the primitive Culture. The only field in which this Culture endured through to the second age (though certainly in a very 'late' form) and is found alive and fairly intact today is north-west Africa. It is the great merit of Leo Frobenius that he recognized this quite clearly, beginning with the assumption that in this field a *whole world* of primitive life (and not merely a greater or less number of primitive tribes) remained remote from the influences of the high Cultures. The ethnologist-psychologist, on the contrary, delights in collecting, from all over the five continents, fragments of peoples who really have nothing in common but the negative fact of living a subordinate existence in the middle of one or another of the high Cultures, without participation in its inner life." (*Decline of the West,* II, 33.)

imaginative more than the scientific mind does not fall within our interest at the moment; Pound sees such influence as the poet registering sensibilities in advance of the specialists. Yeats's *A Vision,* for instance, owes much to Spengler and Frobenius (translated aloud by Pound at Rapallo). Guillaume Apollinaire was inspired early by Frobenius's collection of primitive art, and probably led Matisse, Derain, Vlaminck, and Picasso in that direction. Frobenius had published the first essays on primitive art as art in 1895 and 1897.

Bronislaw Malinowski, evaluating a list of mythologists, discards Frobenius with half a sentence.[14] *The Encyclopaedia of the Social Sciences* does much the same thing. Whatever the cause of the chronic disregard and misrepresentation of Frobenius which has infuriated Ezra Pound for twenty-seven years now, it is evident that both that disregard and misrepresentation are very real.[15] For one of many possible examples, see what Susanne K. Langer, in *Philosophy in a New Key* does with two passages from Frobenius's first attempt in the study of culture morphology, *Aus den Flegeljahren der Menschheit* (1901), translated in 1909 as *The Childhood of Man.* Frobenius was twenty-eight when the book was published; he had made no field trips at the time but had collected primitive art and accounts of primitive life from missionaries and commercial travelers to the extent that he had as firm a basis for ethnographic study as one could expect for the period. Mrs. Langer says:

[14] Bronislaw Malinowski, "Myth in Primitive Psychology," in *Magic, Science, and Religion and Other Essays* (Boston, 1948).

[15] "C. W. Ceram" has pointed out the neglect of African cultures in Toynbee, citing Frobenius as the filler. (*Gods, Graves and Scholars* [New York, 1951], p. 411.)

Frobenius, also a pioneer in the study of primitive society, describes an initiation ceremony in New South Wales, in the course of which the older men performed a dog-dance, on all fours, for the benefit of the young acolytes who watched these rites, preliminary to the painful honor of having a tooth knocked out. Frobenius refers to the ritual as a "comedy," a "farce," and is amazed at the solemnity with which the boys sat through the "ridiculous canine display" . . . . A little later he describes a funeral among the Bougala, in the Southern Congo; again, each step in the performance seems to him a circus act, until at last "there now followed, if possible, a still more clownish farce."

The last quotation, concerning the funeral, is not Frobenius's but Max Buchner's, written in 1880; the former account of the ritual dog-dance is accurately described, the emotional words "farce" and "ridiculous canine display" not eliciting ridicule of the Bengal aborigines' initiation rite but conveying almost soberly the antic preliminary of what Frobenius describes sympathetically as a solemn ceremony. Criticism which neglects twenty-eight years of a man's work, choosing to consider a first book rather than forty-odd later ones, has made of Frobenius also a genuine "man of no fortune and with a name to come." All of this is not to vindicate Frobenius in the eyes of Mrs. Langer or Malinowski; I merely wish to furnish reality for the pervading frustration in Pound's writing over the neglect that Frobenius has suffered in apparently all quarters.

The April 30, 1953 issue of *The Listener,* published by the British Broadcasting Corporation, had an unsigned article on Ifé sculpture lacking mention of Frobenius but referring obscurely and incompetently to his theory of the origin of Nigerian art. Pound could see this obfuscation of science only as a paralysis of communication, as indeed it seems. Frobenius made a thorough and reasonably conclusive study of the Nigerian bronzes and terra cottas from 1910 to 1912, the discovery of the best of them being his achievement; Pound's contention that education suffers from lack of direction and the scholar's ignorance of his own field of reference rings sorely true when tested against such evidence. Pound uses the phrases "Boycott & timelag . . . founded in sin . . ." in protesting the journalistic narrowness of the article on Ifé art. Further notation from Pound's correspondence should register his despair over the neglect of that part of his orthodoxy which we are attempting to understand and to place in relation to his poetry and criticism:

> 13 Mar 1953 "Erlebte Erdteile" 7 vols <u>still</u> <u>un</u>translated they want 'something in the nature of gems.'

> "Childhood of Man" transd in 1910 was where things were when Frob. started . . .

Pound is a year late with the date of the translation, which was by A. H. Keane, vice-president of the Royal Anthropological Institute of Great Britain, and as for "where things were" in 1909, we should note that anthropology did not have at that time, except for the pioneering of Durkheim, Wundt, Frazer, and Boas, the major works it was to have a year later. Malinowski's article, "Anthropology," in the thirteenth edition of the *Encyclopaedia Britannica* commences its survey with the year 1910, omitting Frobenius.

Pound's "at least" five categories of criticism as given in "Date Line. Rapallo Jan 28th, Anno XII," the introductory essay in *Make It New,* clarify his formal approach to Frobenius: criticism in new composition. This is apparently what was intended by the publication of *Guide to Kulchur;* the hortatory letter to Eliot concerning the vital necessity of understanding culture as Frobenius outlines it says as much, and Pound admits that *Guide to Kulchur* is, after a fashion, a work in the manner of Frobenius.

> Even were I to call this book the New Learning I shd. at least make a bow to Frobenius. I have eschewed his term almost for the sole reason that the normal anglo-saxon loathes a highsounding word, especially a greek word unfamiliar. . . . When I said I wanted a new civilization, I think I cd. have used Frobenius' term.
>
> At any rate for my own use and for the duration of this treatise I shall use Paideuma for the gristly roots of ideas that are in action.
>
> I shall leave "Zeitgeist" as including also the atmospheres, the tints of mental air and the idées réçues, the notions that a great mass of people still hold or half hold from habit, from waning custom.
>
> The "New Learning" under the ideogram of the mortar can imply whatever men of my generation can offer the successors as means to the new comprehension. . . .
>
> CH'ING MING, a new Paideuma will start with that injunction as has every conscious renovation of learning.

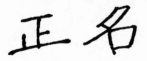

Having attained a clear terminology whereof no part can be mistaken for any other, the student might consider another point raised by Frobenius when interviewed by Dr. Menotti.

"It is not what a man says, but the part of it which his auditor considers important, that measures the quantity of his communication."

"Date Line" next defines the two functions of criticism, "gun sight" and excernment, the latter being both from and toward a study of Frobenius:

> The general ordering and weeding out of what has actually been performed. The elimination of repetitions. The work analogous to that which a good hanging committee or a curator would perform in a National Gallery or in a biological museum;
>
> The ordering of knowledge so that the next man (or generation) can most readily find the live part of it, and waste the least possible time among obsolete issues.

In order to determine just how active Frobenius is as subject in the text of *The Cantos,* an examination of part of Canto LXXIV should serve as a beginning:

> and Rouse found they spoke of Elias
> in telling the tales of Odysseus   ΟΥ ΤΙΣ
>   ΟΥ ΤΙΣ
> "I am noman, my name is noman"
> but Wanjina is, shall we say, Ouan Jin
> or the man with an education
> and whose mouth was removed by his father

                    because he made too many *things*
            whereby cluttered the bushman's baggage
            vide the expedition of Frobenius' pupils about 1938
                                        to Auss'ralia
            Ouan Jin spoke and thereby created the named
                                        thereby making clutter
            the bane of men moving
            and so his mouth was removed
            as you will find it removed in his pictures
                                in principio verbum
                    paraclete or the verbum perfectum: sinceritas

Pound is here implying that W. H. D. Rouse, who, like Victor
Bérard, went over the route of the Odyssean journey in a sail boat,
was working in the manner of Frobenius in discovering the
paideuma—the Homeric culture, having suffered a sea-change,
but sustained by its own vital relation to the people who kept it
living for some 2,800 years—of certain Greek islands where tales
of Odysseus are still to be heard. He has become fused with the
prophet Elias and in some versions his periplus reaches to the
mysterious city of Chicago. Lawrence Durrell has some lively
notes in his *Prospero's Cell* on the metamorphosed version of *The
Odyssey* at Corcyra. This traditional culture of a people Frobenius
called paideuma, "the tangle or complex of inrooted ideas of any
period," a title Pound admits he would have liked to use for his
Guide to Kulchur. The counterpart in Frobenius of Rouse's finding Homer active after a fashion among Greek fishermen is his
early discovery (1904) among the Nigerian culture-groups of
Benin and Nupé of an Issa-tshi, or "Jesus people" who count among

their tribal gods Nassarawa Issa, or Jesus of Nazareth, knowledge of whom came centuries ago from Byzantium, across
Africa.

Having brought to the fore Odysseus, prime hero in many
guises of *The Cantos,* Pound brings with him a strange figure.
Wanjina is partly explained by Hugh Gordon Porteus in his essay
on Pound's handling of the Chinese ideogram.[16] Commenting on
a kind of brash folk etymology to which Pound is prone, Porteus
says, "Thus in one place in *The Pisan Cantos* he actually equates
'Wanjina' (an African rain god out of a Frobenius legend) with
'Ouan Jin' (French transliteration of Chinese for 'literary gent'
—in Wade transcription: *Wen jen*)." Such uncritical equation of
alleged cognates is nothing more than Pound's amateur anthropology in the manner of Frobenius,[17] whose establishing of iconographic and etymological parallels—Altamira and Bulawayo cave
painting, Shango and Poseidon, for example—is one of the initial
shocks in his writing. The wondjina figures, discovered by Sir
George Grey in 1837 and studied, as Pound notes in the passage
in question, by an expedition of Frobenius's pupils in 1938 (the
year of Frobenius's death), are primitive ground drawings in
Northern Kimberly, Australia (not Africa, as Porteus surmises).[18]
That these figures have no mouths interests Pound immensely.
"Ouan Jin"—Pound's metamorphosis of the Australian rain icon
into "the man with an education"—"spoke and thereby created
the named / thereby making clutter/ . . . and so his mouth was

---

[16] "Ezra Pound and His Chinese Characters: A Radical Examination," in *Ezra
Pound: A Symposium,* ed. Peter Russell (New York, 1950).

[17] Pound admits that he made the identification on a basis of "sound only," but
sees no reason why a Chinese loan-word could not be used by Australian aborigines.

[18] See Leonhard Adam, *Primitive Art* (Penguin Books, 1949).

removed." The elliptic transition from Ouan Jin, the mouthless, to the next lines

> in principio verbum
> paraclete or the verbum perfectum: sinceritas

brings the excursion into Australian mythology back around to the epos proper if the nature of the ellipse be seen full force. My guess is that the Pisan preoccupation with the principle of light in Manichaeism—remember Grossetesta, Cavalcanti, and Scotus Erigena—led Pound to another parallel: that of Mani's identification of himself as a man of right reason with the Paraclete, which in turn is identified with "that light which comes from looking straight into the heart" defined by Confucius in the *Ta Hio* as being the sincerity of the wen jen, the man with a knowledge of the good, for Pound equates with a colon verbum perfectum and sinceritas. Further, the ellipse takes its energy from the iconographic paralleling of word, mouth, and logos, the absence of the latter, in accordance with John 16:7, being prerequisite for the appearance among men of the Paraclete, thus equating, seemingly, the mouthless Wanjina with the fertile presence of God in man.

> in the light of light is the *virtù*
>> "sunt lumina" said Erigena Scotus
>> as of Shun on Mt Taishan
> and in the hall of the forebears
>>> as from the beginning of wonders
> the paraclete that was present in Yao, the precision
> in Shun the compassionate
> in Yu the guider of waters   (Canto LXXIV)

It little matters, after so agile a manipulation of ideographs, that the Australian aborigines believe that if their wondjinas had mouths rain would fall without cease and mankind would drown.[19]

The Pisan Cantos represent the *Paradiso* or the beginning of the *Paradiso* of the poem, depending on whether the last section be written. Its title, not yet made public, indicates a final statement of dogma. "My *Paradiso*," Pound says, "will have no St Dominic or Augustine, but it will be a *Paradiso* just the same, moving toward final coherence. I'm getting at the building of the City, that whole tradition. Augustine, he don't amount to a great deal." [20] City and mountain—Taishan, Dioce, and Wagadu—are the paradisical images, "visions," as Pound calls them. The city "whose terraces are the colour of stars" is King Deioces', seven-walled and purgatorially shaped; its description in Herodotus (1. 98) is but inspiration for the city that Pound describes. The other city, Wagadu, "now in the mind indestructible," which

[19] Pound learned of the wondjinas through members of the Forschunginstitut, Douglas C. Fox among them, when they stopped by Rapallo on their way back from the Australian expedition. Wondjina, the son of a god, created the world by speaking the names of objects. Because he began to create too many things, his father took away his mouth. In the passage in Canto LXXVII
> and Tom wore a tin disc, a circular can-lid
> with his name on it, solely:
> for Wanjina has lost his mouth,
the point seems to be that Tom, who was a native servant of a Miss Simpson in New Zealand and went naked save for his name on a disc worn on a string around his neck, displays the totem-power of the *named*: the sacred function of Wondjina still within the culture since the Stone Age. The source is again Fox at Rapallo.

[20] Interview at St. Elizabeth's Hospital, July 17, 1953. Pound also mentioned this date that there will not necessarily be one hundred Cantos ("the length is elastic") and that he finds his *Paradiso* the most difficult part of the poem to write.

blends its image with that of Dioce, is from a Soninke legend recorded in Frobenius's *Monumenta Africana* (*Erlebte Erdteile,*
Vol. VI). Were it not for Pound's disavowal of symbolism in *The
Cantos*—the order of symbolism used by Joyce up to and through
Ulysses specifically—it would appear that these two cities are
symbolic; Alan Neame has suggested beauty and virtue respec-
tively.[21] Pound's intensity of vision and tenseness of structure are
apt to draw from speculative criticism a supposed symbolism
which in fact has not been intended. The line ". . . four giants
at the four corners," coming so soon after the comparisons made
between the philosophers of light, Confucius, Erigena, and Mani,
would, if written by a symbolist rather than an imagist, connect
with the four Atlas figures of Manichaean cosmology. "They were
a vision," Pound has explained, and have nothing to do with Mani.
So with the mountains and the cities: the meaning is ordered
toward an ipse rather than a significat.

The ideographs of the city are as follows:

(1) To build the city of Dioce whose terraces are the colour
of stars

(2) Lute of Gassir. Hooo Fasa

(3) 4 times was the city rebuilded, Hooo Fasa
Gassir, Hooo Fasa,   dell' Italia tradita
now in the mind indestructible, Gassir, Hoooo Fasa,
With the four giants at the four corners
and four gates mid-wall Hooo Fasa
and a terrace the colour of stars

[21] "The Pisan Cantos/An Approach," *The European*, 4.

       pale as the dawn cloud, la luna
            thin as Demeter's hair [22]
       Hooo Fasa, and in a dance the renewal
(4) Cloud over mountain, mountain over the cloud
       I surrender neither the empire nor the temples
                           plural
       nor the constitution nor yet the city of Dioce
       each one in his god's name

(5) "I believe in the resurrection of Italy   quia impossibile est
        4 times to the song of Gassir
             now in the mind indestructible
                        (Canto LXXIV)

(6)   nothing matters but the quality
    of the affection—
    in the end—that has carved the trace in the mind
    dove sta memoria   (Canto LXXVI)

(7)   and Awoi's *hennia*   plays hob in the tent flaps
          k-lakk . . . . . thuuuuuu
        making rain
             uuuh
  2,   7,   hooo
     der im Baluba

---

[22] Note throughout *The Cantos,* particularly the Pisan, the celebration, as here, of the chthonic Demeter religion, basically an agricultural rite (*vide* Aristotle's "Economics begins with agriculture") which serves Pound as counterbalance to the "light descending" principle of the Confucius–right reason–paraclete passages. Pound's efforts to get Zielinsky translated are as lively as those toward a translation of Frobenius.

      Faasa   !   4 times was the city remade,
now in the heart indestructible
           4 gates, the 4 towers
(Il Scirocco è geloso)
                men rose out of χθονος
                Agada, Ganna, Silla
                         (Canto LXXVII)

(8)   Whither go all the vair and the cisclatons
       and the wave pattern runs in the stone
       on the high parapet (Excideuil)
       Mt Segur and the city of Dioce
       Que tous les mois avons nouvelle lune   (Canto LXXX)

Two Soninke legends, "Gassire's Lute," which has given Pound
his imagery for a city "in the mind," and "The Rediscovery of
Wagadu," will have to be familiar to the reader who wants to be
aware of the total meaning of the city-mountain images in the
Pisan Cantos.

The legend of Gassire's lute begins:

    Four times Wagadu stood there in all her splendour, four
times Wagadu disappeared and was lost to human sight: once
through vanity, once through falsehood, once through greed,
and once through dissension. Four times Wagadu changed
her name. First she was called Dierra, then Agada, then Ganna,
then Silla. Four times she turned her face. Once to the north,
once to the west, once to the east, and once to the south. For
Wagadu, whenever men have seen her, has always had four
gates: one to the north, one to the west, one to the east, and

one to the south. These are the directions whence the strength
of Wagadu comes, the strength in which she endures no matter whether she be built of stone, wood, or earth, or lives but
as a shadow in the mind and longing of her children. For,
really, Wagadu is not of stone, not of wood, not of earth.
Wagadu is the strength which lives in the hearts of men and
is sometimes visible because eyes see her and ears hear the clash
of swords and ring of shields, and is sometimes invisible because the indomitability of men has overtired her, so that she
sleeps. Sleep came to Wagadu for the first time through vanity,
for the second time through falsehood, for the third time
through greed, and for the fourth time through dissension.
Should Wagadu ever be found for the fifth time, then she will
live so forcefully in the minds of men that she will never be
lost again, so forcefully that vanity, falsehood, greed and dissension will never be able to harm her.

Hoooh! Dierra, Agada, Ganna, Silla! Hooh! Fasa!

Every time that the guilt of man caused Wagadu to disappear she won a new beauty which made the splendour of
her appearance still more glorious. Vanity brought the song
of the bards which all peoples (of the Sudan) imitate and
value today. Falsehood brought a rain of gold and pearls.
Greed brought writing as the Burdama practise it today, and
which in Wagadu was the business of the women. Dissension
will enable the fifth Wagadu to be as enduring as the rain
of the south and as the rocks of the Sahara, for every man
will then have the Wagadu in his heart and every woman a
Wagadu in her womb.

Hoooh! Dierra, Agada, Ganna, Silla! Hoooh Fasa! [23]

"Leave blanks," Pound has pleaded, "for what you don't know."
The Cantos being unfinished, Frobenius a relatively late encounter
and his full impact needing far more demonstration than can be
given here, the blanks are necessarily large, but not without material indicative of what will fill them. It is easy to say that Pound
has begun to see culture through Frobenius's eyes, as it can be
said that he saw sculpture through Gaudier's and Brancusi's or
China through Ernest Fenollosa's, but he has gone further than
perspicacity, has opened interest to his sources with one hand and
with the other created in their spirit (but not in their wake);
Bérard could not have given us a new epic containing Odysseus,
nor Frobenius Wagadu in relation to Confucius and Dante, nor
Fenollosa *Cathay*. The belabored anecdotes of finding the car of
Dis and Persephone and of always finding subterranean water
near rock pictures registers an excitement over a kind of intelligence which Pound has consistently admired (Agassiz and the
fish, for instance); the periplus must be seen before lesser men
can make a map. Frobenius's was a periplus experience; academic
anthropology has made the maps which Pound finds deadly dull.

Perhaps the primary enthusiasm for Frobenius caught spark
when Pound saw in him a kinship of method which he had developed independently, "to learn the nature of error"; Pound's
early studies of medieval Italy and Provence and of Greece, China,
and the United States bear identity with Frobenius's insight into
individual African cultures: an establishing of paideumic structure

[23] Frobenius and Fox, *African Genesis*, pp. 109–10.

whereby the culture can be seen at its peak and ruin and its parts
traced in diffusion. That Frobenius could demonstrate forces in the
disintegration of a culture naturally interested Pound immensely,
for the collapse of cultures within China, the United States, and
Greece ("They have brought whores for Eleusis," he says in Canto
XLV) has been searchingly treated in *The Cantos*. Pound's attitude
toward and acceptance of Frobenius, at the writing of *Guide to
Kulchur,* shows not so much a wariness of his adventurous specu-
lations (the Atlantis theory, for instance) as an intuitive enthusiasm
for his peculiar sharpness of insight:

> The question whether I believe Frobenius right or wrong
> in any given point seems to me frivolous. He cd. be wrong in
> 40 points and still bear gifts above price.
>
> That a man find the car of Persephone in a German burrow
> is already a mental property. That one's roots are not a disease
> but parts of a vital organism is worth feeling.

That Pound wants to remove from around Frobenius—and
Alexander Del Mar and Brooks Adams—a "conspiracy of silence,"
that he claims pre-eminence for Frobenius as an anthropologist,
or that a new learning should stem from *Erlebte Erdteile* is no
more germane to an understanding of *The Cantos* than other
pedagogical impulses behind the fabric of history and mythology,
though we know them to be behind the "quality of affection" that
has merged the images of two fabulous cities, Median and African,
into an image of a Paradise of the mind. Frobenius wears the
mask of Odysseus in *The Cantos;* the early and pivotal motif of
πολλῶν δ'ἀνθρώπων ἴδεν has brought him among the heroic personae of the epic; later and more thorough study of *The Cantos*

and what role Frobenius will play in the *Paradiso* to come should establish his position, alongside Confucius, Dante, and Homer, within the hard core of orthodoxy, "now in the mind indestructible."

SISTER M. BERNETTA QUINN, O.S.F.

The Metamorphoses of Ezra Pound *

Among the many approaches to *The Cantos* of Ezra Pound which illuminate its design, not the least fruitful is the pursuit of the metamorphic theme. It is indeed surprising that so little critical attention has been given to this aspect of the poem, since Pound has clearly stated on several occasions that metamorphosis is one of the two major themes used to effect continuity in the long work. The best-known expression of his intentions is that confided to William Butler Yeats, who, although he misunderstood what Pound meant by fugal structure, has left us in "A Packet for Ezra Pound" an excellent account of how the metamorphic principle was to be applied. Recording a conversation with Pound on *The Cantos,* Yeats writes:

> There will be no plot, no chronicle of events, no logic of discourse, but two themes, the descent into Hades from Homer, a Metamorphosis from Ovid, and mixed with these medieval or modern historical characters (*A Vision,* pp. 4–5).

Pound, eager as always to drive home his meaning, then scribbled on the back of an envelope a diagram based upon a photo-

* This essay is an extension of "Ezra Pound and the Metamorphic Tradition," which appeared in the *Western Review*, xv (Spring, 1951), 169–81.

graph hanging on the wall; it was of a Cosimo Tura decoration in three compartments, the upper representing the Triumph of Love and the Triumph of Chastity; the middle, the Zodiac; and the lower, certain events in the time of Tura himself. Referring to this design, Pound explained his plan of using as one theme (ABCD) the descent to Hell, as a second (JKLM) metamorphosis; repeating these; then reversing the first (DCBA) to fit changing circumstances; introducing archetypal persons (XYZ) and a fifth structural unit, symbolized by any letters that never recur, to stand for contemporary events; finally setting all sorts of combinations of ABCD, JKLM, XYZ, DCBA whirling together. Yeats then shows how this algebraic analysis relates to the Tura design:

> The descent and the metamorphosis—ABCD and JKLM— his fixed elements, took the place of the Zodiac, the archetypal persons—XYZ—that of the Triumphs, and certain modern events—his letters that do not recur—that of those events in Cosimo Tura's day.

That this design is not a discarded hope but one realized in practice can be verified by a careful examination of the whole of *The Cantos* published thus far, though the evidence is not convincing if one looks only at a single block of the verse. Further proof that Pound did not change his mind about the basic components of his poem is contained in a 1927 letter which he wrote from Rapallo to his father, Homer Pound, in which he explained its major themes:

> A.A. Live man goes down into world of Dead
> C.B. The "repeat in history"

B.C. The "magic moment" or moment of metamorphosis,
bust thru from quotidien into "divine or permanent
world." Gods, etc.

Five years after that, he says in a letter to John Drummond that
the three planes in *The Cantos* are "the permanent, the recurrent,
the casual." In 1937, he writes to John Lackay Brown: "There *is*
at start, descent to the shades, metamorphoses, parallel (Vidal-
Actaeon)." The appearance of the Pisan section with its frequent
echoes of the ABCD and JKLM themes indicates that the original
scheme is still being followed, and subsequent Cantos will un-
doubtedly make the pattern unmistakable.

Significantly, Pound's enthusiasm for Ovid, particularly as that
poet has been translated by the Elizabethan, Arthur Golding, is
unequaled among his fiery espousals of ancient or contemporary
authors. His letters and criticisms are filled with injunctions to his
fellow-artists to go out and read the *Metamorphoses,* exalted by
him as by the Middle Ages (though for different reasons) to a
rank analogous to that of the Scriptures. He places it among the
five literary works requisite for culture, in such high company
as the Confucian Odes, Homer, the *Divine Comedy,* and the Plays
(*Culture,* p. 236). Twice he calls Golding's version the most beautiful book in the English language (*The A B C of Reading,* pp.
44 and 115) and considers the editor, W. H. D. Rouse, the person
who has given him more pleasure than any other man living,
because he is "the man who made Golding's *Ovid* available"
(*Polite Essays,* p. 125).

Pound's interest in the *Metamorphoses* is twofold: artistic and
philosophical. Repeatedly he emphasizes the fact that Golding
created a new Ovid, and states that a knowledge of how he did so

is indispensable to an understanding of English or any other division of literature. After quoting at length in *The A B C of Reading* from the episode of Cadmus, Pound continues:

> I apologize for the cuts in the story, but I cannot give a whole book of the Metamorphoses here, and I do not honestly think that anyone can know anything about the art of lucid narrative in English, or let us say about the history of the development of English narrative writing (verse or prose) without seeing the whole of the volume ("The XV Bookes of P. Ouidius Naso, entytuled Metamorphosis, translated oute of Latin into English meeter, by Arthur Golding Gentlemen") (pp. 114–15).

Any English department, he writes to Sarah Perkins Cope in 1934, "is a farce without it." Like Chapman, the translator Golding, whose version had reached seven editions by 1597, was an authentic poet in his own right, contributing many beautiful effects not in Ovid, just as Ovid added things not in Greek literature.

But besides beauty, the *Metamorphoses* contains a great treasury of wisdom; it is a depository of truth which could be registered in this form and in no other. While foreign editor for *Poetry,* Pound instructed Harriet Monroe, whom he apparently enjoyed shocking, that she should inform the American public as follows concerning his beliefs: "Say that I consider the Writings of Confucius, and Ovid's *Metamorphoses* the only safe guides in religion" (*Letters,* p. 183). Ovid presents a world of permanent values, of absolutes, one in which Pound also is at home and into which he introduces us whenever he makes allusion in *The Cantos* to gods and goddesses of classical cultures.

Pound has taken as a subject for criticism another book of metamorphoses, widely popular but far inferior to Ovid—the *Golden
Ass* of Lucius Apuleius. *The Spirit of Romance* contrasts Apuleius
with Ovid, much to the disadvantage of the former:

> To find out how these metamorphoses of Apuleius differ
> from preceding Latin, we may compare them with the meta-
> morphoses of Ovid. Both men write of wonders, and trans-
> formations, and of things supernatural.
>
> Ovid—urbane, sceptical, a Roman of the city—writes, not in
> florid prose, but in a polished verse, with the clarity of French
> scientific prose. . . . His mind, trained to the system of empire,
> demands the definite. The sceptical age hungers after the defi-
> nite, after something it can pretend to believe. The marvellous
> thing is made plausible, the gods are humanized, their annals
> are written as if copied from a parish register; the heroes
> might have been acquaintances of the author's father (pp.
> 6–7).

Then Pound goes on to describe admiringly the Ovidian treatment of the legend of Daedalus and Icarus, stressing its verisimili-
tude, and setting it against the extravagance and once-upon-a-time
quality of Apuleius, whose floridity preceded Gongorism and the
prolixity of medieval romance. The chief reason why Pound is
drawn to the Augustan poet rather than to the author of the Cupid-
Psyche story is given in one sentence, which serves also to illuminate the use of Ovidian techniques in *The Cantos:* "Ovid, before
Browning, raises the dead and dissects their mental processes; he
walks with the people of myth; Apuleius, in real life, is confused
with his fictitious hero." However, despite this expression of dis-

approval of Apuleius, at least one critic, Allen Tate, has seen resemblances between Pound's poetry and the *Golden Ass*: "The Cantos are a sort of *Golden Ass*. There is a likeness, but there is no parallel beyond the mere historical one: both books are the product of worlds without convictions and given over to hard pragmatism" (*Reactionary Essays on Poetry and Ideas*, p. 50).

To understand what role transformation plays in *The Cantos*, one might consider the doctrine of changes as it affects things, then ideas, and finally the creative act itself, since this is the order in which these three occur in relation to the artifact. First, metamorphosis of things. Of this, Pound says in "Affirmations," "The undeniable tradition of metamorphosis teaches us that things do not remain the same. They become other things by swift and unanalysable process." That he means this statement quite literally is apparent from his interpretation of evolution in the postscript which he wrote for his translation of Remy de Gourmont's *The Natural Philosophy of Love:*

> I believe, and on no better ground than that of a sudden emotion, that the change of species is not a slow matter, managed by cross-breeding, of nature's leporides and mules. I believe that the species changes as suddenly as a man makes a song or a poem, or as suddenly as he *starts* making them, more suddenly than he can cut a statue in stone, at most as slowly as a locust or long-tailed Sirmione false mosquito emerges from its outgrown skin (p. 174).

The suddenness with which May breaks upon a countryside and the rapid quenching of day's-end gold and cerise are among the natural phenomena involved in Pound's "swift and unanalysable process." This going-forward of the universe has not escaped comment by his favorite Oriental sages; it is part of the process meant by Confucius in Book VII of the *Analects:* "He said: keep your mind (will, directio voluntatis) on the process (the way things function)." One of Pound's irritable spots is impatience with those who regard the tenets of Mencius and Confucius as static, refusing to pay attention to their frequent use of verbs indicating change and renewal; he says so vehemently in a *Criterion* essay, "Mang Tsze," wherein he includes the ideogram for metamorphosis, used again in Canto LVII. Among Western thinkers Heraclitus put the same concept into the two words, "all flows," which appear repeatedly in the Cantos, besides being paraphrased in *Hugh Selwyn Mauberly*. Water symbolism, meant to give concreteness to this idea, is a persistent motif, worthy of a separate essay.

Pomona, wooed in Canto LXXIX by Vertumnus, the deity of the seasons whose very name means "he who changes," is used by Pound to represent the cycle of the year; Nature's recovery from apparent death in the triumph of spring and its annual surrender to winter is concretized further in the Cantos by three classical myths. The first, employed merely as an incidental figure, is that of Atthis: "And many things are set abroad and brought to mind / Of thee, Atthis, unfruitful" (Canto v). Atthis, the Phrygian shepherd beloved of Cybele who emasculated himself under a fir tree, his spirit at death passing into the tree and (as in the Hyacinthus, Adonis, and Narcissus legends) flowers springing from his blood, stands in Pound's mind for a negative attitude toward the sex instinct. He opposes the Atthis-Adonis mentality to a Mediterranean one in *Make It New,* dividing culture upon that basis:

By 1934 Frazer is sufficiently digested for us to know that opposing systems of European morality go back to the opposed temperaments of those who thought copulation was good for the crops, and the opposed faction who thought it was bad for the crops (the scarcity economists of pre-history). That ought to simplify a good deal of argument. The Christian in being Christian might at least decide whether he is for Adonis or Atys, or whether he is Mediterranean (p. 17).

In the following year, he comments in a letter to Henry Swabey on the Atthis element "in all Anglo-Education" (*Letters,* p. 264).

The second myth relates the history of Adonis, introduced in Canto xxiii with a reference to his having died virgin; Canto xlvii devotes more space to him, using the refrain Καὶ Μοῖραιτ' Ἄδονιν six times. The anemones Venus caused to rise from his blood are Pound's "flower from the swift seed," "Four banners to every flower." An analogue to the Greek story—the legend of the Babylonian god Tammuz, whose blood was said to stain the waters of a certain river in spring flood times—is incorporated into this Canto, which combines the myths thus: "The sea is streaked red with Adonis." The last of these fertility types is Proserpina, spoken of in the first Canto, hinted at in Canto xxi, and mentioned several times in the Pisan section, especially in connection with the pomegranate. In Canto lxxiv her name is linked with the Sirens, her attendants who were metamorphosed after her abduction by Pluto.

Others kinds of metamorphoses observable in the world about us are the formation of rocks and the much faster decomposition of the human body. Pound has given explicit treatment to the latter, so frequently a subject of poetry, in Cantos xxvii, xxxvii, and

LXXX. The first of these begins: "Formando di disio nuova persona / One man is dead, and another has rotted his end off"; the second refers to such decay as the descent to plant life; the last dramatizes disintegration in this quatrain with its overtones of Victorian verse:

> Nor seeks the carmine petal to infer;
> Nor is the white bud Time's inquisitor
> Probing to know if its new-gnarled root
> Twists from York's head or belly of Lancaster

The Ash Wednesday liturgy of the Catholic Church, which gives tangible form to the belief that man has originated from the dust and must return to it (*Memento, homo quia pulvis es, et in pulverem reverteris*) is reflected in the three Cantos dealing with the Cadmus story, first alluded to in XXVII: "Me Cadmus sowed in the earth / And with the thirtieth autumn / I return to the earth that made me." The myth is picked up again in XXXIII ("whether serpents' teeth sprang up men . . .") and is concluded in LXXVII ("men rose out of χθόνος" and again, "the forms of men rose out of γέα"). Canto XXVIII begins with a similar picture, except that God the Father has taken the place of the pagan deities:

> And God the Father Eternal (Boja d'un Dio!)
> Having made all things he cd.
> think of, felt yet
> That something was lacking, and thought
> Still more, and reflected that
> The Romagnolo was lacking, and
> Stamped with his foot in the mud and
> Up comes the Romagnolo

Eventually these men out of earth return to their mother, Gea, by the nature of the process, and are gathered together in Orcus, the shadowy land of the dead.

A related subject is metempsychosis, mentioned by Pound in Canto LIX as well as in the first of the Pisan Cantos, and expounded much earlier in his lyric "Histrion":

> No man hath dared to write this thing as yet,
> And yet I know, how that the souls of all men great
> At times pass through us,
> And we are melted into them, and are not
> Save reflexions of their souls.
> Thus am I Dante for a space and am
> One Francois Villon, ballad-lord and thief
> Or am such holy ones I may not write,
> Lest blasphemy be writ against my name;
> This for an instant and the flame is gone.

The personae device leaps to one's mind at the reading of this poem, Pound's series of forms which project themselves into the translucent golden sphere of the ego—Odysseus, Sordello, the Cid, Actaeon, Vidal, Sigismundo, and the rest. Ovid's Renaissance translator, Golding, has anticipated "Histrion" in: "For soules are free from death. Howbeet, they leaving ever-more / Theyr former dwellings, are receyved and live ageine in new." Certainly no reader of the Roman poet could escape this extension of the metamorphic theme, as Herman Fränkel points out in *Ovid: A Poet between Two Worlds*: "Furthermore the theme gave ample scope for displaying the phenomena of insecure and fleeting identity, of a self divided in itself or spilling over into another self" (p. 99).

One's entire life is, in a sense, a struggle for complete self-realization. The artist, with his highly receptive sensibility, is more intensely aware of this search, which Pound describes in "Vorticism," a 1914 contribution to the *Fortnightly Review*. He speaks ruefully of how, as soon as one is able to say "I am this," he ceases to be so —a fact making it necessary to go on looking for one's true self discarding all the masks afforded by the workings of the imagination (p. 463). Eliot, five years later in the *Athenaeum,* described Pound's method as just such a throwing-aside of mask after mask ("The Method of Mr. Pound," p. 1065).

The relation between the terms *personae* and *personality* is an interesting one: Pound's practice has been to use the first for exploration and definition of the second:

> I began this search for the real in a book called *Personae,* casting off, as it were, complete masks of the self in each poem. I continued in a long series of translations, which were but more elaborate masks.

The essay on vorticism from which this passage is taken appeared near the beginning of his career—he has since created many fascinating personae to express, among other things, the mystery of self. The process is well illustrated by the Cosimo Tura diagram which Pound drew up for Yeats, in relation to which these masks are to be considered as the XYZ theme. It is as if a soul (X or Y or Z) went from body to body, throughout the ages, retaining in each transmigration its original character. X, Y, and Z, however, are not the souls of ordinary human beings, but composites, archetypes: X_1 becomes X_2, which changes to X_3 in an inspired metempsychosis which lends unity to the entire poem. As D. S. Carne-Ross points out: "It is a basic principle of *The Cantos* that all related characters can merge, or meet, into one another" (*An Examination of Ezra Pound,* p. 159).

The archetypes fall into three major classes: heroes, heroines, and enemies (male or female) of the life of value. Among the heroes are found both good rulers of their people and artists of integrity: Odysseus; Kung, Hanno; Roland; the Cid; Provençal troubadours like Vidal, Sordello, William of Poitiers, Piere de Maensac, Savairic Mauleon, Arnaut Daniel; Cavalcanti; Sigismundo Malatesta and Borso d'Este; Pisanello, Titian, Carpathio; American leaders such as John Adams, Jefferson, Van Buren; Pietro Leopoldo; Henry James; Mussolini. In these men, however, the good is not unmixed with evil. Pound's heroines include Helen of Troy, Eleanore of Aquitaine, Ignez de Castro, Lady Soresmunda, Isotta degli Atti, the Marchesa Parisina d'Este, Cuinizza— all of them women whose flesh enshrined a gleam of the eternal beauty. Among the villains are Chi Hoang Ti; Ou-heou; Franz Joseph; Hamilton and Marshall; Churchill; Krupp, Metevsky, and others who reap the evil gains of usury. The gods and goddesses, too, and mythological figures of lower rank (Circe, Terreus, Lycabs) blend one into another, so that the sun-god may be called Mithras, Phoebus, Apollo, or Helios; Diana may be referred to as Artemis or Titania.

Pound introduces the idea of metempsychosis into his attitudes toward actual as well as fictive characters; always impatient of confinement to the present, he rejoiced in the impression of reincarnation which his young sculptor-friend, Gaudier-Brzeska, awakened in him, an impression of being with someone out of Castiglione, or with the subject of a Renaissance painting (*Gaudier-Brzeska,* p. 50).

Another indication of his interest in metempsychosis is his loving

study of the Rimini bas-reliefs, those magnificent carvings in which
Agostino di Duccio and other quattrocento artists united their
genius to perpetuate the passionate devotion of Sigismundo, Lord
of Rimini, for his third wife, Isotta. An extreme of metempsychosis is reached in a figure of Saint Michael in one of the chapels
in the temple, where the Archangel has the face of Isotta. Pound
has also called attention in his criticism to the metempsychosis
which informs the long eulogy, *Isottaeus,* written by the court poet
Basinio in honor of his patron's wife (*Criterion,* XIII, 496).

   Not only does this transformation operate from soul to soul,
but also in empathetic fashion between man and non-human nature. Relationships, truths otherwise unsuspected, are revealed
through entrance into the life of one's environment. In his brief
poem, "The Tree," Pound brings up to date the several Ovidian
tales of persons turning into trees (Daphne, the Heliades, Baucis
and Philemon, Dryope, Cyparisse, Myrrha, the Thracian women,
the shepherd of Appulia); the central thought is expressed in these
lines:

> I stood still and was a tree amid the wood,
> Knowing the truth of things unseen before;
> Of Daphne and the laurel bow
> And that god-feasting couple old
> That grew elm-oak amid the wold.

The reverse of this transformation is presented in the popular
lyric, "A Girl," wherein a tree becomes a girl, the tree, however,
being employed metaphorically to symbolize her lover:

> The tree has entered my hands,
> The sap has ascended my arms,

> The tree has grown in my breast—
> Downward,
> The branches grow out of me, like arms.

Shortly after quoting from Pound's "The Tree," Joseph T. Shipley in his *Trends in Literature* has this to say about an important movement in modern aesthetics:

> This inevitable identity of the individual with his surroundings is made the basis of one of the time's most credited theories of beauty. Anything is beautiful, according to the doctrine of Einfühlung, or empathy, that draws us into its being. Thus Socerian says, "We have only one way of imagining things from the inside, and that is putting ourselves inside them." Bergson declares that the spectator must become actor. Lotze asserts that we accomplish the feat: "We project ourselves into the forms of a tree, identifying our life with that of the slender shoots that swell and stretch forth, feeling in our souls the delight of the branches that drop and poise delicately in mid-air" (pp. 271–72).

All this, as well as Pound's lyric, might be described as the imagination exercised to the height of its capacity.

The underlying use which Pound makes of the metamorphoses of things might best be classified as an epistemological one, divided into theories of self-knowledge and extra-ego knowledge. Only by accommodating apperception to the nature of things—a nature epitomized by Golding in "In all the world there is not that that standeth at a stay / Things eb and flow, and every shape is made too passe away"—can we attain truth. We must be willing to admit that our version of reality needs constant revision if it is to remain valid. Moreover, the subject as well as the object is continually changing; what served yesterday as an equation for one's personality, or any fragment of it, is no longer satisfactory today. Only the man who grasps this psychological situation and keeps voluntary pace with his metamorphoses will succeed as a human being.

Besides using metamorphosis as a way of knowing reality, Pound has taken over the principle as a means of uniting the parts of a poem already more than six hundred pages long. In a review of Ford Madox Ford's novel, *Parade's End* (a review given over chiefly to a discussion of Ezra Pound's innovations in structure), Ambrose Gordon explains this technique as follows:

> For it seems likely that there actually is something inherent in local clarity itself—in the very sharply defined image or, for that matter, idea—which sets it off from all that is exterior to it, which prevents a "flow." Thus to mediate between individual brilliant moments,—in a poem or a novel—something rather like a movie "fade in" or, more accurately, a montage is what is required—if you will, a metamorphosis (*Furioso,* VI, 85).

To understand what Gordon means here, one needs only to call to mind the way in which one cinema scene is worked into another through the wizardry of the camera, without destroying the illusion, and then think of any single Canto as this comparison applies to it.

Canto I, for example, contains only one such metamorphosis since the bulk of it is straight translation from the eleventh book of the Odyssey, via Andreas Divus; that change occurs at the very end, where Ulysses, having consulted Tiresias in the underworld, sails off to the shores of Circe. Suddenly we find ourselves with Aphrodite, still in the Homeric world (the concluding lines refer to the Second Hymn) but in a new sequence of timeless moments, equally luminous. Similarly, in Canto XVI the hideousness of the usurers' hell gives way to the bright serenity of Pound's purgatory only to relapse again into the inferno of war. This is not simply progress by association of feeling or ideas; the distinctness, precision, and knife-edged clarity for which Pound has ever striven war against the vagueness of the reverie method.

The way in which metamorphosis effects transitions between juxtaposed "brilliant moments" stands out more vividly in those Cantos containing several classical mutations; an excellent example is Canto II. After an introduction including three waterscapes— Oriental waters churned by So-Shu (King of Soku), a northern sea where seals frolic along with the transformed daughter of the Irish King Lir, and the harbor where the old Greeks at once admire and condemn Helen—this second Canto moves from the story of Tyro taken in love by Poseidon in the form of her river-god husband Enipeus into the story of Bacchus and the Tyrrhenian pirates. So smoothly is this done that one does not even realize that the sea touching Scios has replaced the waters where Tyro was seduced. After a lengthy paraphrase of Golding's Bacchus-Acoetes episode, the sea changes to that wherein Ileuthyeria, metamorphosed to coral, gleams in ivory stillness. Pound follows this image with another glimpse of So-Shu and then turns the scene once more into the Tyro-Poseidon setting.

Gordon puts his finger on the success of such a method when he goes on to say:

It is ultimately a metaphorical device, an affair of identity; for it may quite plausibly be argued that the present local object or situation—in a poem, in drama—always by parody or analogy tends to suggest another object or situation which is not present; e.g., when one is with Claudius one is also with Hamlet senior and vice versa.

Thus Itys and Cabestan (Canto IV) stand in a metaphorical relationship, as do Actaeon and Vidal in the same Canto; De Tierci and Menelaus (Canto V); both of these rejected husbands with Richard Saint Boniface in the next Canto; Eleanore and Helen (Canto VII). Even the perversions of the positive characters are bound into the whole by their distortions of the pattern; Kung, maker of order, immediately precedes the causers of disorder punished within the filth of Canto XIV.

In addition to treating the metamorphoses of things, Pound takes up those of ideas, the effectiveness of which depends upon their renewal. This is crystallized in the title of his 1934 collection of essays, *Make It New,* a direction quoted twice in Canto LII, which also contains the corresponding ideogram. Emperor Tching Tang of the Chang dynasty had this motto painted on his bath tub, the emperor who in Pound's translation of the *Ta Hio* is described as having "kept his gaze fixed ceaselessly upon this bright gift of intelligence which we receive from the sky" (p. 11). In the ideogram the signs for *new* and *sun* are combined so as to give what might literally be translated as "New, day by day new." Rejuvenation is achieved by clothing the basic thought in fresh particulars, the vitality of which has not been worn down by familiarity.

In *Culture,* Pound labels the forma, the concept immortal (p. 152). This concetto, separable from its materialization only logically, travels through time, seizing upon successive embodiments, each of which shows it in its power, an idea in action. "Nothing is new and all good is renewal," Pound declares in a *Criterion* essay. The jungle, to which Richard Eberhart has compared the Cantos (*QRL,* v, 180), is the best example of such reforming; as Canto xx puts it,

> Glaze green and red feathers, jungle,
> Basis of renewal, renewals;
> Rising over the soul, green virid, of the jungle,
> Lozenge of the pavement, clear shapes,
> Broken, disrupted, body eternal,
> Wilderness of renewals, confusion
> Basis of renewals, subsistence,
> Glazed green of the jungle

This order out of confusion, incidentally, parallels the cosmos-out-of-chaos with which Ovid begins his *Metamorphoses.* Canto xxv, after speaking of the meadows of Phlegethon, phrases the theory thus: "And thought then, the deathless, / Form, forms and renewal, gods held in the air." Just as metempsychosis presupposes a fixed number of souls, so this view of thought binds one to an absolutist position, a World of Ideas, as it were, which changes only in its phenomenal aspects. This is a rigid commitment, but one from which Pound does not shrink:

> I mean or imply that certain truth exists. Certain colours exist
> in nature though great painters have striven vainly, and

though the colour film is not yet perfected. Truth is not un-true'd by reason of our failing to fix it on paper. Certain objects are communicable to a man or woman only "with proper lighting," they are perceptible in our own minds only with proper "lighting," fitfully and by instants (*Culture,* p. 295).

To make the truth of these ideas perceptible, then, is Pound's aim in following the precept of the Chinese emperor.

One such idea requiring to be made new—an idea which appears in various guises throughout the centuries—is that it is vicious to twist the will, to defraud one's fellow man, as in usury. To get this pivotal truth across, Pound uses two major stories of transformation as well as a few minor ones. The first is that of Circe; Hugh Kenner calls her the most clearly defined character in the first half of the poem. Allen Tate goes even further:

> Mr. Pound's world is the scene of a great Odyssey, and everywhere he lands it is the shore of Circe, where men "lose all companions" and are turned into swine . . . And ironically, being modern and a hater of modernity, he sees all history as deformed by the trim-coifed goddess (*Reactionary Essays on Poetry and Ideas,* p. 48).

Tate's comment, however, is hardly valid as a description of *The Cantos.* While it is true that the world it represents is the scene of an Odyssey, not all the points of landing are comparable to the shores of Circe—certainly not the ardent re-creations of Chinese, Renaissance, or early American civilization. Moreover, to call Pound a hater of modernity—Pound, who has championed so many artists ahead of their age—would require a very special definition of that term.

The initial Canto, which Pound himself describes in *Make It New* (pp. 137–43) as a close translation from the Odyssey, says nothing of Circe's sorcery, though it mentions the trim-coifed goddess five times. Canto xxxii hints at the mutations she effected: "and thus are become as mere animals / . . . whether in a stye, a stable or in a stateroom." Canto xxxix is largely devoted to her; it speaks of "Lions loggy with Circe's tisane"; it gives her parentage (Helios and Perseis) as well as the name of her sister (Pasiphae); it also provides an account of the magic diet she prepared for the victims of her craft:

> First honey and cheese
> > honey at first and then acorns
> Honey at the start and then acorns
> honey and wine and then acorns

In Canto lxxiv, Pound goes back to this central myth, clearly connecting it with usury, that lust for earthly goods which turns men into swine:

> every bank of discount is downright iniquity
> > robbing the public for private individual's gain
> nec benecomata Kirkê, mah! κακὰ φάργακ' ἔδωκεν
> neither with lions nor leopards attended
> > but poison, veleno
> in all the veins of the commonweal

Fragments of the story occur in Greek, Latin, English; the last Canto to be published thus far includes a few lines of the Circe myth in Italian, as if the poet wished to bring home in as many ways as possible the wretched evil of moneylending. In the "e poi io dissi alla sorella / della pastorella dei suini" Canto LXXXIV he echoes the "and at sunset la pastorella dei suini / driving the pigs home, benecomata dea" of Canto LXXVI. Greed is one of the dangers of modern life, just as it was one of the obstacles facing Ulysses and his men on the way home to Penelope.

By translating this keystone truth into a vivid fiction, Pound hopes to reinstate it in the minds of his contemporaries; besides the Homeric-Ovidian method of doing so, he utilizes the medieval craze to discover an elixir which would change base metal into gold, that dream which brought ruin to so many scientists. Marco Polo is quoted in Canto XVIII as reporting of Kublai's empire: "I have told you of that emperor's city in detail / And will tell you of the coining in Cambaluc / that hyght the secret of alchemy." By spelling the Chinese emperor's name Kahn instead of Khan, Pound telescopes time—not, after all, a factor of great importance in his realm of values. The medieval Khan's scheme for issuing paper money on pearls and other valuables and the modern Kahn's profits from usury, a way of creating money out of nothing, are thus contrasted. Another Chinese ruler, Hien of Tang, Pound informs us in Canto LVII, died seeking the fatal elixir, "seeking the transmutation of metals / seeking a word to make change." This is immediately followed by the ideogram for metamorphosis.

This ideogram is an interesting one. It consists of a radical meaning "the spoken word," in center position, bordered on either side by one signifying "silk as a raw material," and all three are placed over a fourth sign meaning "a literary thing, form, the finished product, anything with art in it." The latter originally consisted of a meeting of two lines, a cross effected by design—of a very simple type, of course, but still art. Thus the concept is rooted in a concrete analogy based upon one of the best-known forms of metamorphosis: caterpillar–chrysalis–butterfly; and beyond that, it is based upon the exquisite silks for which the Orient is famous. The complete ideogram is defined in the *Concise Dictionary of Spoken Chinese* prepared by Yuen Ren Chao and Lien Sheng Yang as meaning "to change."

The other important development of the usury theme is the Bacchus-Acoetes myth, adapted from the poem of Ovid, via Golding; it is the most complete example of Poundian metamorphosis. The differences between Canto II and the two older accounts are chiefly those of condensation and idiom, besides the devices of anaphora and repetition of entire lines as these occur in the latest version. As always in his translations, Pound wishes to preserve the spirit rather than to attain literal accuracy. Colloquial terms such as "loggy," "cum' along lad," "aye," "racket," make the incident come alive, while the interruptions of direct address create an eyewitness effect. The rhythms of conversation are managed with a sureness of poetic line to make this passage one of the finest in the Cantos. The "god-sleight" (wonderful compound!) is given much more space in Pound than in the two sources, indicating that his absorption in the moment of rapid mutation is perhaps even greater than that of Ovid, about whom he says: "No Greek was so interested in the magical instant as was Ovid" (*Criterion,* I, 155).

Wherever Pound thinks he can make the transformation more real to the sentient man, he does not hesitate to add ideas not present in the sources; for instance, out of "stetit aequore puppis / haud aliter, quam si siccum navale teneret," which Golding translates as "The ship stoode still amid the Sea as in a dustie docke," he derives "Ship stock fast in sea-swirl," retaining in five simple words the motion of the water around the magically "frozen" ship. One of his best contributions is "grapes with no seed but sea-foam," a reference to their divine origin which has no equivalent in Ovid and Golding. The picture of jungle cats materializing out of the void is accomplished by appeals to all five senses, with each variant expression of the metamorphosis adding to the irresistible cumulative effect. The order of sense-impressions here is handled with amazing rightness: first, just hot breath on the ankles of Acoetes as if from invisible nostrils, then "Beasts like shadows in glass," at two removes from reality. The immaterial character of these Dionysiac symbols is a high achievement, for which almost none of the credit is due to Pound's models.

Acoetes represents the man of a straight will, of integrity: the merchant seaman who will not betray his god. Contrasted with him are the sailors of perverted wills, whose hunger for worldly riches causes them to break all laws of truth or justice in order to obtain gold. About this, Golding moralizes: "so sore mennes eyes were blinded / Where covetousenesse of filthie gaine is more than reason minded." Their sins are such as are symbolized by the monster Geryon, emblem of Fraud, who figures in Cantos XLIX and LI, as well as in the *Divine Comedy*. Bacchus does well to punish by reduction to the bestial level human beings as depraved as are those who try to live by bread alone.

In addition to these expanded transformations, Pound employs as a criticism of usury that of Midas (Cantos XXI, LXXVII, LXXVIII), whose avarice was so dreadfully rewarded. He also uses the shield of Athena (Justice) in order to win an exit for his dramatic character from the usurers' hell described in Canto XV:

> Prayed we to the Medusa,
>> petrifying the soil by the shield,
> Holding it downward
>> he hardened the track
> Inch before us, by inch,
>> the matter resisting,
> The heads rose from the shield,
>> hissing, held downwards

Departing from the realm of antique transformations but keeping to a similar condemnation, Pound in Canto LXXIV tells about an experience in Tangier, when he saw a snake long as a man's arm bite the tongue of a fakir. From the blood thus drawn, dirty straw stuffed into the fakir's mouth was ignited; this "something" from no adequate cause corresponds perfectly to the poet's view of usury, called in the same Canto "lending / that which is made out of nothing."

A second crucial idea, given many guises in the poem, is that beauty is extremely hard to possess, as Danaë, Actaeon, Salmacis, the historical Piere Vidal, among others, found out to their sorrow. Danaë's love for Jupiter had been merely a gasp between the clichés of daily life; Pound speaks of her in Cantos IV and V as the bride awaiting the god's touch, awaiting the golden rain. The myth of Actaeon is told at greater length, in the fourth Canto. Pound weaves into his tragedy the lycanthropy of the troubadour Vidal, who dressed in wolf-skins for the love of Lady Loba de Peugnautier (whose name means wolf), even allowing himself to be hunted by dogs and beaten by shepherds. In both these accounts the hunter, paradoxically, becomes the victim, the second being a grim parody of the first in that Vidal is a self-appointed victim. In *Exultations* Pound had published a Browningesque monologue, "Piere Vidal Old," wherein the troubadour, driven through the mountains of Cabaret by hunters with hounds, tells his own story. The last line of this lyric ("Ha! this scent is hot!") shows how completely Vidal had been conquered by his wolf-delusion.

In two lines, Canto IV brings together three famous pools in a way that transcends space and time: Vidal is shown reciting Ovid as he stumbles through the Provençal forest: " 'Pergusa . . . pool . . . pool . . . Gargaphia, / Pool . . . pool of Salmacis.' " Pergusa was the pool near which Proserpina had been playing just before her rape; Gargaphia, that wherein Diana was bathing; Salmacis, that named after the water-nymph who was enamored of the beautiful but cold Hermaphroditus and fused with him into a double-sexed being. Just as the water-bodies of Canto II are one, so are these. Immediately after the two lines quoted, Pound summarizes the transformation of Cygnus into a swan, as Ovid relates it in Book XII: "The empty armour shakes as the cygnet moves"; thus he depreciates further the significance of chronology. Economy and rhythmic invention are characteristic of Pound's version, drawn out of Ovid's "arma relicta videt; corpus deus aequoris albam / contulit in volucrem, cuius modo nomen habebat" and Golding's "But nought he in his armor found. For *Neptune* had as tho / Transformed him too the fowle whose name he bare but late ago."

A third idea which turns from one mythical context into another is that love must be free. If, as Hugh Kenner thinks, Circe dominates the first half of *The Cantos,* the figure emerging as primary from the entire work is Venus, the goddess of love, presented under the several titles of Aphrodite, Cythera, Hathor, and Primavera. How necessary Pound considers this virtue may be seen in the letterhead he uses for some of his correspondence: *"J'ayme donc je suis."* No external forces can control this value, not even the hardships of the Pisan D. T. C. In the last analysis, nothing truly good comes from violence, whether in public or private relationships. An ancient myth which powerfully exemplifies this axiom is that of Procne and her sister Philomela. Canto IV blends this story with the equally horrible one from the Provençal vidas, in which a banquet of her lover Cabestan's heart is served to Lady Soremonda by her husband, Sir Raymond of Castle Rossillon, an atrocity which causes the young wife to commit suicide. Pound's delicate combination of these analogues is worthy of quotation:

> Ityn!
> Et ter flebiliter, Ityn, Ityn!
> And she went toward the window and cast her down,
>   "All the while, the while, swallows crying:
> Ityn!
>   "It is Cabestan's heart in the dish."
>   "It is Cabestan's heart in the dish?
>   "No other taste shall change this."
> And she went toward the window,
>   the slim white stone bar
> Making a double arch;
> Firm even fingers held to the firm pale stone;
> Swung for a moment,

>   and the wind out of Rhodez
>   Caught in the full of her sleeve.
>   . . . the swallows crying:
>   'Tis. 'Tis. Ytis!

The union of the legends is accomplished, among other ways, by gradually altering the name of the child-victim in the Greek tale: the Latin accusative Ityn (also a union of Itys and Cabestan) > It is > 'Tis > Ytis. Another phase of Pound's skill in blending is the resemblance of these sounds to swallow song. An echo from Horace makes the allusion even richer—Ityn flebiliter gemens in *Carmina* IV. xii. 5. One is surprised that the name of the castle, Rossillon (which suggests nightingale), finds no place in the poem. Toward the close of the Canto the joined ideas occur again: "Cabestan, Terreus, / It is Cabestan's heart in the dish." Echoes also appear later, in Cantos LXXVII and LXXXII. Lust, then (a perversion of the will just as avarice is), and cruel jealousy lead only to suffering, often of the most brutal kind.

Daphne, like Philomela, is a woman whose lover seeks to compel, not entreat, affection. Her mutation, which Ovid tells with the liveliest of details, has long fascinated Pound. In *Hugh Selwyn Mauberly* he writes: "Daphne with her thighs in bark / Stretches toward me her leafy hands"; ten years earlier the speaker in "La Fraisne" changes the traditional laurel to dogwood: "By the still pool of Mar-nan-oltra / Have I found me a bride / That was a dogwood some syne." "The Girl" is, of course, based on this myth. In *The Cantos* it is treated only obliquely; Canto II describes an analogue, which reads like a popular belief concerning the origin of coral:

And of a later year,
> pale in the wine-red algae,
If you will lean over the rock,
> the coral face under wave-tinge,
Rose-paleness under water-shift,
> Ileuthyeria, fair Dafne of sea-bords,
The swimmer's arms turned to branches,
Who will say in what year,
> fleeing what band of tritons,
The smooth brows, seen, and half seen,
> now ivory stillness.

The incident is picked up again in Canto xxix: "(fleeing what band of Tritons)." Ileuthyeria is a personification of freedom, the meaning of the Greek word. At the conclusion of Canto ii, the fauns (symbol of masculine fertility) chide Proteus (the ever-changing one) for being on the side of this composite woman; in triumph the frogs (symbolic of metamorphosis) sing against the fauns. Just one other reference to Daphne herself occurs in *The Cantos*—in Canto lxxvi, where her name is coupled with that of the quattrocento painter, Botticelli.

More subtle compulsion of love is given triple presentation in the wooing of Tyro, Alcmene, and Thetis; in each of these court-ships "god-sleight," craft, replaces force. Neither of the first two women seems to have relished the substitution of a god for her husband—the stratagem of disguise employed by the deities—to judge from Pound's Canto lxxiv:

between NEKUIA where are Alcmene and Tyro

. . . .

femina, femina, that wd/ not be dragged into paradise by the
hair

For sheer loveliness of imagery, nothing in the Cantos surpasses
the description of Tyro's possession by Neptune, which combines
the color-words blue-gray glass, glare azure, sun-tawny, sun-film,
black azure, hyaline, bright welter, buff sands, glass glint, grey,
salmon-pink in such a way as to create an unforgettable amalgam
of shade and radiance.

That the third, Thetis, did not want to be dragged *out* of paradise by her hair, the Roman poet implies in these lines; "tum
demum *ingemuit,* 'neque' ait 'sine numine vincis' / exhibita estque
Thetis" (italics mine). According to Ovid, Peleus beheld the sea-
nymph Thetis as she slumbered in her Thessalian cave and determined to have her for his bride; she, equally resolved that he
should not, transformed herself from bird to tree to tigeress.
Peleus, however, prayed to the sea-deities, in response to which
petition Chiron, the Centaur, advised him to hold the maiden fast,
no matter what form she might assume. The Peleus-Thetis story
is not developed in Pound; he merely glances at it in Cantos XXXVI
and LXXVI, as a way of reinforcing his treatment of modes of love
and violence. Canto LXXIV alludes to another mortal unwilling to
love a deity: Tithonus, whom Aurora changed to a grasshopper
when she saw the sad consequences of Jove's gift to him of eternal
life without eternal youth.

The story of a somewhat similar courtship, that of Venus and
Anchises, forms the bulk of the Second Homeric Hymn to Aphrodite, from which Pound quotes in Canto I. It is unlike the Tyro-

Alcmene situation in that Anchises recognizes the divinity of his
visitor, even though she tells him that she is the daughter of Otreus,
King of Phrygia; he most willingly agrees to the union, which
bears fruit in the hero Aeneas. Aphrodite announces herself in her
assumed identity at the close of Canto XXIII; two Cantos later she
repeats, "King Otreus, my father"; a shadowy allusion to the story
occurs in the first of the Pisan group ("as by Terracina rose from
the sea Zephyr behind her / and from her manner of walking
/ as had Anchises"); finally a striking particular is given in Canto
LXXVI:

> or Anchises that laid hold of her flanks of air
> drawing her to him
>> Cythera potens, κύθηρα δεινά
> no cloud, but the crystal body
>> the tangent formed in the hand's cup
> as live wind in the beech grove
>> as strong air amid cypress.

Since this plan was devised by Love herself, the outcome was free
of reluctance.

Each metamorphosis of an idea, then, presents a change within
a change. First of all, Pound uses the various transformations
(Circe, Actaeon, etc.) as exempla, ways of setting ideas in action.
Like any great teacher, he realizes that concepts of goodness are
effective only in so far as they are in operation; like any great
artist, he knows that only what has been actuated (i.e., changed
from potency to act) can be an object for contemplation.

The last type of metamorphosis to be considered is that which

Pound equates with the artistic process. Nowhere has he better explained what he means by this identification than in this passage from a 1915 *New Age* essay, "Affirmations":

> The first myth arose when a man walked sheer into "nonsense," that is to say, when some very vivid and undeniable adventure befell him, and he told someone else who called him a liar. Thereupon, after bitter experiences, when he said that he "turned into a deer," he made a myth—a work of art that is—*an impersonal or objective story woven out of his emotions,* as the nearest equation that he was capable of putting into words. That story, perhaps, then gave rise to a weakened copy of his emotions in others, until there arose a cult, a company of people who could understand each other's nonsense about the gods (italics mine; p. 246).

After this definiton, he expostulates about using myths for purposes other than this type of communication—for political or ethical good, allegorically or as a fable. One speculates as to what he might say about the moralized Ovids so common in the late Middle Ages and early Renaissance.

This aesthetic theory suggests scholastic definitions of form, substance, and accident. The artist has the form in his mind before he begins work: "as the sculptor sees the form in the air / before he sets hand to mallet" (Canto xxv). This is not, however, the Platonic notion of forms as types but a unique concept. Rather than changing the substance while retaining the accidents, Pound transforms the accidents while keeping the substance as it was. Thus Dante's epic and the *Analects* may be substantially the same though their verbal manifestations (the accidents) may vary. In *Make*

It New Pound significantly remarks that Guido Cavalcanti used the whole poem to define an accident (p. 360).

Not only in literature does this principle of metamorphosis operate but also in sculpture. One of Pound's favorite periods in sculpture is the fifteenth century, an era in which artists regarded stone as sacred and endowed with forms which struggled to be expressed. This is the idea that animates Canto LXXIV: "stone knowing the form which the carver imparts it / the stone knows the form." Pound treats this aspect of sculpture at greater length in *Make It New*:

> We might say: The best Egyptian sculpture is magnificent plastic; but its force comes from a non-plastic, i.e. the god is inside the statue . . . The god is inside the stone, *vacuos exercet aera morsus*. The force is arrested, but there is never any question about its latency, about the force being the essential, and the rest "accidental" in the philosophic technical sense. The shape occurs (p. 349).

This Latin quotation from Ovid's seventh book of the *Metamorphoses* was also used by Pound in 1920 as prologue for the second part of *Hugh Selwyn Mauberly,* the fourteenth section of which concludes:

> Mouths biting empty air,
> The still stone dogs,
> Caught in metamorphosis, were
> Left him as epilogues.

Adrian Stokes devotes much space in his book, *Stones of Rimini,* to the distinction between carving and modeling—between letting a form imprisoned in stone emerge and imposing a form from without—relating his critical pronouncements to the exquisite bas-reliefs of Agostino di Duccio which ornament the Tempio Mala-testa. The several Cantos dealing with the Tempio, as well as scattered references, are evidences of Pound's passionate interest in this quattrocento wonder of sculpture. Stokes identifies Isotta with Diana herself (p. 252), one of the dominant figures in the Cantos, appearing also under her Greek title of Artemis—the feminine principle (moon) as opposed to the masculine principle (sun); the rose (Isotta's emblem) to the elephant (Sigismundo's emblem); Yang to Yin, as the Chinese express the opposition. A most striking representation of Diana's power is the Duccio re-lief, "Influxion of the Moon," wherein waves achieve the stasis of mountains and trees are rooted in the swirling deep as moonlight softens, even obliterates, the differences between the elements.

Stokes also has a fascinating book on another Italian city, Venice, which might be called the city of metamorphosis and which forms the heart of one of the most beautiful descriptions in *The Cantos* (xvii). Though Venice is not mentioned by name, the details given, plus the line "Thither Borso, when they shot the barbed arrow at him" (a misfortune which Canto x tells us happened to Borso D'Este in Venice), warrant considering the scene as Venetian:

> A boat came,
> One man holding her sail,
> Guiding her with oar caught over gunwale, saying:
> "   There, in the forest of marble,
> "   the stone trees—out of water—

" the arbours of stone—
" marble leaf, over leaf,
" silver, steel over steel,
" silver beaks rising and crossing,
" prow set against prow,
" stone, ply over ply,
" the gilt beams flare of an evening"
Borso, Carmagnola, the men of craft, *i vitrei,*
Thither, at one time, time after time,
And the waters richer than glass,
Bronze gold, the blaze over the silver,
Dye-pots in the torch-light,
The flash of wave under prows,
And the silver beaks rising and crossing.
      Stone trees, white and rose-white in the darkness,
Cypress there by the towers,
      Drift under hulls in the night.

Canto xxv adds further details to the picture of this city, the Renaissance "Regina del Mare."

In *Venice: An Aspect of Art,* Stokes lets his imagination dissolve the barriers between the limestone carvings of Venice and the life these resemble, likening the balustrade-supports of the old prison's windows to penguins; referring to sea-birds as stones released from the buildings they once ornamented; calling the food given to the pigeons of Saint Mark's an offering to the stones themselves (p. 6). In his earlier volume on Rimini he had already pointed out the metamorphic nature of Venice: "In Venice the world is stone . . . There, the lives of generations have made

exteriors, acceptable between sky and water, marbles inhabited by
emotion, feelings turned to marble" (pp. 16–17). More than ten
years later, he redefines this sense of transformation which is
peculiarly Venetian:

> We have seen a principle of interchange inspiring Quattro
> Cento architecture; we have seen that Venice herself inspires
> a lively sense of poetry, of metamorphosis, of interchange, of
> inner in terms of outer (p. 55).

This concept, which Stokes in his rather florid style takes pages
to establish, is crystallized by Pound in a few lines near the end of
Canto xvii:

> And shipped thence
> > to the stone place,
> Pale white, over water,
> > known water,
> And the white forest of marble, bent bough over bough,
> The pleached arbour of stone

That Pound is familiar with the work of this critic of quattrocento
art is evident from his review of *Stones of Rimini,* published in the
Criterion in 1934. Stokes, on his part, affirms on page 26 of this
book on Venice that he has been inspired in his quattrocento research by the Sigismundo Cantos of Pound.

In painting, too, the metamorphic principle applies; e.g., the
drawing forth of forms from the air of the poet's imagination, so
wonderfully expressed by Sandro Botticelli (whose Dafne is
mentioned in Canto lxxvi) in his "Venus Rising from the Sea,"
its background starred with aerial flowers of miraculous origin.

Pound might almost be describing this picture in Canto xxvii:
"But in sleep, in the waking dream, / Petal'd the air," and again,
" 'The air burst into leaf.' / 'Hung there flowered acanthus.' "
Canto lxxx credits Sandro Botticelli with knowing secrets of his
art never suspected by Velasquez, who was "lost in the brown
meat of Rembrandt / and the raw meat of Rubens and Jordaens."

Metamorphosis also functions in music. Canto lxxv, except for a
few lines of introduction, consists entirely of the transcription for
violin by Gerhart Münch (*per metamorfosi,* as the manuscript
says) of Clement Janequin's bird-song chorale. (The special meaning of metamorphosis in music is the repetition of a musical figure
or idea with modifications giving it a new character.) Pound's
comments in his criticism and letters on this "Canzone degli
Uccelli" invariably present this work as a unit of eternal beauty
which has traveled down through the ages, seizing upon various
media to manifest itself. Through Pound's influence, after correspondence with the Princess Edmond de Polignac to obtain the
score, the canzone was presented at Rapallo on October 10, 1933.
The following passage from *Culture* points out its metamorphic
nature:

> Janequin's concept takes a third life in our time, for catgut
> or patent silver, its first was choral, its second on the wires of
> Francesco Milano's lute. And its ancestry I think goes back to
> Arnaut Daniel and to god knows what "hidden antiquity"
> (p. 152).

Later in the same book, while again tracing the life of Janequin's
birds back to Francesco da Milano and to Arnaut, Pound says:
"One of the rights of masterwork is the right of rebirth and re-

currence" (p. 251). The inclusion of the Janequin score in the midst of *The Cantos* is no irrrelevance, as those who adhere to the "rag-bag" school of Poundian criticism declare; rather it strengthens the several allusions to actual birds forming ever-new ideograms on the electrically charged wires of the Pisan D. T. C., as James Blish has brought out in the *Sewanee Review* (LVIII, 219). Canto LXXV hints to us that the birds in LXXVII and LXXXII are writing on their wire staff a musical score, truly a "Canzone degli Uccelli."

Furthermore, though this is not evident at present, Canto LXXV has been prepared for in one of the Cantos omitted from the New Directions edition (those between LXXI and LXXIV); in a section from those which Pound sent to his Japanese friend, Katue Kitasano, this line occurs: "We have heard the birds praising Janequin." It should be remembered, too, that Pound naturally desires the reader to play, or have someone else play, the Canto, so that the ear may reinforce that sense of permanent loveliness which the poem as a whole repeatedly opposes to corrupted values. This is a type of positive metamorphosis set against the degradation of the Circean kind.

Allied to the art of original creation is that of translation. Pound's versions of Latin, Tuscan, Provençal, and Chinese literature prove him a translator worthy to be ranked among the finest, despite outcries of purists. The root meaning of "translate," to change from one condition into another, sets Pound's translations securely within the metamorphic tradition. All men when they exercise the act of cognition are imitators, reproducing in the intellect the material object. The real translator is not, of course, a copyist, but rather an imitator. As Pound puts it in *Culture,* "Golding made a new Ovid" (p. 249). The translator's work consists in causing a thing to recur in matter different from the original. The excellence of the result depends upon the exactness with which he works out the ratio of A : B : : C : D (original vision : poem : : his own vision : translation). If the sides balance, the metamorphosis is acceptable as art.

Pound's most extensive Canto experiment in this type of metamorphosis is Canto xxxvi, the first eighty-four lines a very close rendering of Guido Cavalcanti's canzone, "Donna mi priegha," an alternate translation of which is included in *Make It New* (pp. 353–56). Pound's choice of Cavalcanti is not due entirely to his strong conviction that the Italian poet has much to teach artists of the twentieth century, nor to his intense pleasure in Cavalcanti's songs. The reason why so much space is given to this lyric is this:

> In Guido the "figure," the strong metamorphic or "picturesque" expression is there with purpose to convey or to interpret a definite meaning. In Petrarch it is ornament, the prettiest ornament he could find, but not an irreplaceable ornament, or one that he couldn't have used just about as well somewhere else (*Make It New*, p. 351).

What does Pound mean by "the strong metamorphic or 'picturesque' expression"? Like Guido, and unlike Petrarch, he uses his words in an exact sense, and here to refer to a truth so important that when he told it to T. E. Hulme, the latter exclaimed, after reflection, that he had never read in any book or heard any man say a more interesting thing (*Make It New*, p. 361). He means that Guido, preoccupied with sophisticated points of analyses as to what goes on inside a lover, devised imagery which would take the abstract definition of an emotional situation out of the realm of logical discourse and into the world of breathing, rejoicing, suffering men and women: which would turn the science of psychology (long before it was so called) into the art of poetry. Just as one idea is utterly discrete from all others (the selection of the connotatively right words safeguarding this), so only one rhythm will suffice to render the unique emotion which matches the idea. In the introduction to his Cavalcanti translations, Pound states in a most explicit and uncompromising way the requisites for ideal translation:

> As for the verse itself: I believe in an ultimate and absolute rhythm as I believe in an absolute symbol or metaphor. The perception of the intellect is given in the word, that of the emotions in the cadence. It is only, then, in perfect rhythm joined to the perfect word that the two-fold vision can be recorded. I would liken Guido's cadence to nothing less powerful than line in Blake's drawing (p. xxi).

The problem in translating Cavalcanti, then, is to retain the substance while replacing one set of accidents with another. This is not the problem in translating such a poet as Baudelaire, where (for ugly rather than, as in Petrarch, for pretty effect) many figures may be substituted for the original one (*Imaginary Letters,* p. 49).

Ideograms, the units of Chinese literature, are constantly being "made over" in the later Cantos. Hugh Kenner compares Pound's translations from the Chinese to "Mr. Eliot's metamorphic processing of St. John of the Cross, the Ferrar community, the Gouvernor, his childhood memories, Dante and a rose-garden" (*Hudson Review,* III, 122). Although it is harder for the average reader to judge this side of Pound than it is to evaluate Eliot's mutations, an unbiased study of the Chinese characters as these appear in *The Cantos* reveals that they add richness, visual interest, and scope to the work, not obscurity, since they are nearly always accompanied by English equivalents.

A branch of Poundian translation most pertinent to this essay is the work he has done on the Noh plays, based upon Ernest Fenollosa's studies in Japanese drama. As early as 1917, Pound had published, working on Fenollosa's unfinished drafts, *"Noh" or Accomplishment: A Study of the Classical Stage of Japan.* The plot of one of the plays in this collection, "Awoi No Uye," is completely metamorphic. The lovely Awoi, married to Genji Yugawo, is so jealous that her own passion appears to her, first in the form of the Princess Rakujo, her rival, then in the guise of a demon or "hannya." Pound explains these two transformations as follows:

> The passion makes her [Awoi] subject to the demon-possession. The demon first comes in a disguised and beautiful form. The prayer of the exorcist forces him first to appear in his true shape, and then to retreat.
>
> But the "disguised and beautiful form" is not a mere abstract sheet of matter. It is a sort of personal or living mask, having a ghost life of its own; it is at once a shell of the princess, and a form, which is strengthened or made more palpable by the passion of Awoi (pp. 196–97).

Just before this analysis Pound has said: "Western students of ghostly folk-lore would tell you that the world of spirits is fluid and drifts about seeking shape." Such a view is particularly intriguing when considered in relation to his personae technique.

Ezra Pound, in conclusion, writes of the metamorphoses of things, making the changes real, available to the sentient man. He gives us the metamorphoses of ideas—e.g., the evil of usury, the difficulty of beauty, the unwisdom of violence—by embodying them in the shifting histories of Circe, of the seamen who tried to deceive Bacchus, and of other figures from classical poetry. He describes the metamorphosis of the creative act, showing how it operates in sculpture, painting, music, literature. If he is able to complete his poetic restatement of the metamorphic theme as it informs *The Cantos,* he will have as valid a right as had Ovidius Naso to predict:

> And tyme without all end
> (If Poets as by prophesie about the truth may ame)
> My lyfe shall everlastingly bee lengthened still by fame.

A Man of No Fortune

Perhaps the most frequently heard complaints against *The Cantos* of Ezra Pound are that it appears to be formless and that it is made unnecessarily difficult because of Pound's apparently unfathomable literary and historical allusions. In addition, it has been said that sections of *The Cantos* are dull and verbose. Particularly is this criticism made of the Chinese history Cantos (LIII–LXI) and, somewhat less often, of the John Adams Cantos (LXII–LXXI). It may well be argued that Pound does not attain in either of these sections the incisiveness and vigor of the Malatesta Cantos (VII–XI). But whether or not these sections detract from the movement of the poem is not at issue here. Accepting the apparent difficulties of *The Cantos,* how is one to read it? How is one to superimpose upon it enough of form to make it seem, at least on one level, intelligible?

I should like to suggest the following conclusion and approach: *The Cantos* can best be read as a modern *Odyssey,* following with varying degrees of exactness the experience of Odysseus as Ezra Pound sees it. The narrator of the poem follows the trail of Homer's wanderer, seeking the way home.

Many critics have explained that *The Cantos* follows a pattern somewhat similar to that of Dante's *Divina Commedia*. They point, justly, to the *Commedia's* division into cantos, and speak of a three-fold separation of *The Cantos* into something much like Dante's *Inferno–Purgatorio–Paradiso* triptych. Further, they note that Pound has spoken of a poem of one hundred cantos, the same number Dante wrote for his *Commedia*.

To offer some bolstering to this thesis, there is the explanation Pound himself made to his father in a letter dated April 11, 1927. There Pound speaks of three fugal components that will wind through *The Cantos:*

A. A. Live man goes down into the world of the Dead
C. B. The "repeat in history"
B. C. The "magic moment" or moment of metamorphosis, bust through from quotidien into "divine or permanent world." Gods, etc.

This tripartite scheme has its parallel in the division Dante constructs. One sees, correspondingly, the underworld (*Inferno*), the mountain (*Purgatorio*), and the heavens (*Paradiso*). And as far as the construction of *The Cantos* is concerned, there is a parallel to be observed and followed in the state of mind of the narrator and observer.

But there is an important difference: in the *Commedia* it is very clear who, what, and where the narrator is. He is Dante, a medieval man, at home in a medieval world ordered by the Christian myth. In *The Cantos* there is no presupposed Christian myth as guide. One must search for another myth. And that myth, set in the first Canto, is the myth of Odysseus, the hero who wishes to return home but cannot return until he has suffered and learned through that suffering. But far more important than the construction is the identification of the person who sees and tells in *The Cantos*. The narrator is Ezra Pound as Odysseus, and his Cantos relate the education of Ezra Pound, the modern man, as Homer's poem relates the education of Odysseus.

The window through which this identity becomes clear is Canto XXXIX, which sets forth the core of the *Odyssey* and of *The Cantos*. Canto XXXIX is about four characters, Elpenor, Circe, Eurilochus, and Penelope, who assume vital importance in both the *Odyssey* and *The Cantos* as their significance is understood.

I would suggest that in Canto XXXIX Elpenor and Eurilochus [1] embody alternatives Odysseus may choose as he stands before Circe, who tells him he must go to Hades to seek directions home from the shade Tiresias. Passive Elpenor (man-destroying passion) and aggressive Eurilochus (man-destroying intellect) are shown as aspects of Odysseus' own nature from whom he learns, as in the *Odyssey*, to strike the middle way. Both appear in Canto I, which sets the stage for the listener, Odysseus-Pound, as he stands at the fosse hearing the tales of the dead and awaiting the advice of Tiresias which will lead him home.

Let us consider Canto XXXIX, divided according to the four characters.

Elpenor ("Desolate. . . . vocem," lines 1–36)

Elpenor was the member of Odysseus' crew who fell from the roof of Circe's house, and who met Odysseus when Odysseus and his men entered the underworld. Elpenor was "the youngest of us

---

[1] In Greek, Elpenor (ἐλπίς, *hope for* and ἀνήρ, *man*) means the man who hopes the future will turn out all right without his having to act. Eurilochus (εὐρύ, *wide* and λοχος, *snare*) means the man of widespreading snares.

all, one not so very valiant in war or steady in mind" (*Odyssey* x. 552–53). It is he who speaks as the Canto opens on a scene of lavish, perverted voluptuousness. We first see Elpenor lying on the roof of Circe's house, befuddled and dreaming. We then see him as one of the crew approaching the enchantress's house to be turned into swine. The picture is one of unrestrained passion, both sexual and of the stomach. Circe is identified as the daughter of the Sun, whose sister, Pasiphae, became maddened with lust and copulated with a bull, bringing forth that monster, the Cretan Minotaur. Circe is, to Elpenor and the men-swine, "Venter venustus, cunni cultrix, of the velvet marge." The association of Circe with Pasiphae stresses the metamorphosis of passion into degeneration, which results if passion is allowed to pass beyond its allotted bounds:

> Spring overborne into summer
> late spring in the leafy autumn

"KALON AOIDIAEI" ("the beauty of her singing," *Odyssey* x. 227) is the bewitching song of Circe, which wooed the crew into her house to be transformed into swine. The metamorphosis is again pointed up:

> First honey and cheese
> honey at first and then acorns

These lines emphasize the appetite which allowed Circe to change the crew from men, who ate honey and cheese, to swine, whose diet is acorns. Elpenor speaks languidly, underscoring the metamorphosis of the "ver novum" of the *Pervigilium Veneris* into "late spring in the leafy autumn."

The Elpenor section ends with a quotation from Ovid (*Meta-morphoses* XIII. 538–9) : "illa dolore obmutuit, pariter vocem." The line refers to Hecuba as she suffers the final calamity wrought by Paris' unrestrained passion for Helen, which caused the Trojan War. In Ovid, Hecuba's last living child, Polydorus, is washed ashore a corpse. The old queen stands transfixed with grief, and after slaying her son's murderer, gives way to her hysteria and is metamorphosed to a wolf who goes shrieking over the plains. Elpenor's overindulgence has brought him to the metamorphosis, and its extremity does him to death as he tumbles from Circe's roof in a drunken stupor.

Circe (Greek passage, lines 37–41)

The scene of passion suddenly ends, and there follows the passage from the *Odyssey* (x. 490–5) in which Odysseus, after a year spent in Circe's bed, hears the goddess tell him he must, to get home to Ithaca, go to Hades and seek advice of the soothsayer Tiresias. This is the Tiresias who lived both man and woman, and was struck blind by Hera for judging from that experience that in bed a woman's pleasure is greater than a man's. As recompense, Zeus, who won the wager with his fiery wife, gave Tiresias the everlasting power of prophecy. Thus the Greek passage places us at a point just before *The Cantos* opens. In Canto I Odysseus and his crew are on the way to Hades, having followed Circe's directions. They sail under Circe's tutelage:

> Circe's this craft, the trim-coifed goddess

One must realize that Circe is not merely a witch, but part of the scheme of life. She is "cunni cultrix," a goddess. While she turned the crew into swine, Eurilochus balked; fearing danger, he refused to enter her house, thus denying the metamorphosis. She also failed to transform Odysseus, who with the help of moly, withstood her magic and overpowered her. But Odysseus did, of his own free will, lie with her for a whole year. Thus he neither denied nor succumbed to the metamorphosis, but assimilated it.

Circe's advice is here given in Greek, with no translation, signifying that Pound as Odysseus does not comprehend the full import of her advice. It is as though she spoke to deaf ears in this case, the ears of the man who refused to unbend to her, Eurilochus.

Eurilochus ("When Hathor . . . . boat yet?" lines 42–65)

In the Eurilochus section the key lies in the man who refuses to undergo the metamorphosis in any way. Eurilochus' hardness and his bodyless, physically passionless attitude bring destruction on him when he holds stubbbornly to them. The section opens with Hathor, Egyptian sun-goddess, bound in a box and afloat on the sea. Here the sun-goddess is enslaved and powerless, in direct opposition to Circe's sway over the passionate Elpenor. In this Eurilochean section we shall find that this parallel with the Elpenor section continues—recurring images are altered to conform with the cautious, aspiring Eurilochus; intelligence is perverted instead of lust.

The Italian—"Che mai da me non si parte il diletto"—comes from Dante's *Paradiso* (XXIII. 129), where the redeemed form a crown of light about Mary, singing "Regina Coeli." This is an entirely different kind of singing from Circe's KALON AOIDIAEI— that of a too intellectual divine love as opposed to the call to a too sensual pleasure. And the Virgin Mary is another type of divinity

from "cunni cultrix"; Dante is drawn to redemption through contemplation of an ideal love, Beatrice. "Fulvida di folgore" (*Paradiso* xxx. 62) portrays a river of light "intra due rive / dipinte di
mirabil primavera." This spring and these banks exist quite removed from "late spring" and "the velvet marge" which holds
"Venter venustus." The "due rive" hold the Church Triumphant,
a far cry from Elpenor's sexual passion.

Then comes the picture of Eurilochus, who enters "with Glaucus
unnoticed." Glaucus (Ovid *Metamorphoses* xiii. 898–xiv. 74) also
had his run-in with Circe. Having eaten a strange grass which
made him playfellow with the gods, he loved Scylla. But Circe,
here an evil enchantress, turned her thoughts to Glaucus and,
jealous of the mortal Scylla, turned her to a beast from the waist
down. Both Glaucus and Eurilochus spurn Circe and the passion
of "cunni cultrix," not recognizing her as the goddess who takes
the edge off Odysseus' hubris. Eurilochus refuses to enter Circe's
swinesty—"nec ivi in harum / nec in harum ingressus sum." He
denies her bed, maintaining his overhaughty eminence.

"Eurilochus, Macer" ("Macer" recalls irresistibly Julius Caesar's
remark about Cassius: "Yon Cassius hath a lean and hungry
look") would be better off had he entered the swinesty, where he
would have had at least good acorns. As it is, he becomes the
victim of Poseidon, who would have done in Odysseus too, had
"the man of many devices" not attained reverence from Circe and
the journey to Hades.

Circe prepared him for his journey:

> "I think you must be Odysseus. . . .
>   feel better when you have eaten. . . .
> Always with your mind on the past. . . .

Circe's words underscore Odysseus' Eurilochus alternative—he is too cautious to commit himself, to break down and yield to the metamorphosis which can save him. Odysseus has been guilty of hubris, and Circe lets him know he had better soften a little. He does, but up to this point he has not "Been to hell in a boat yet."

Eurilochus here is the mirror which reflects the Odysseus who craftily devised the Wooden Horse to sack Troy; who unreasonably sacked the Cicones in his warriorlike homeward voyage; who, in his pride, told Polyphemus his name and address, thus bringing down the wrath of the Cyclops' father, Poseidon; who reached for his sword to cut off Eurilochus' head when that worthy tried to keep the rest of the crew from going to Circe's house after half the men had been turned to swine. This Eurilochus is the destructive side of Odysseus' nature, able in war; he is as much a perversion of intelligence as Elpenor is a perversion of passion. Both are "late spring in the leafy autumn," so to speak. It was Eurilochus who forced Odysseus to put in at Thrinacia, the isle of Circe's father, Helios, where the sun-god's flock pastured. It was Eurilochus who instigated the murdering and eating of the sun-god's sacred cattle, thus bringing destruction to the ship and the crew before they reached Ithaca.

Odysseus underwent at Circe's house the experience which altered him, preparing himself for the NEKUIA, or journey to the underworld. Had he refused to enter Circe's bed he would have clung to the Eurilochus alternative and would not have been in the passive mood which opened his heart to the words of Tiresias, thereby to absorb the wisdom of the Land of the Dead. Without that "education," Odysseus would never have reached Ithaca, his home.

Penelope ("Sumus . . . flame," lines 66–105)

The last part of Canto xxxix shifts to the female and portrays real sexual union between man and woman, with the proper ritual. The music is that of the virgins sacred to Artemis, the "Puellaeque canamus" who dance "To the beat of the measure." "Ver novum" of the Elpenor section no longer is "overborne into summer," but the real spring, "Betuene Aprile and Merche / with sap new in the bough." Spring is "made new" (Pound's favorite Chinese maxim), and the god is made by sexual union with the reverent man. At the end of the Canto, what before appeared metamorphosed into perversion shines now in the blush of its earthy and human perfection.

> His rod hath made god in my belly
> Sic loquitor nupta
> Cantat sic nupta

At the end Penelope, Odysseus' perfect wife, blossoms in full splendor. She sings—not Circe's KALON AOIDIAEI calling men to debauchery, nor the heavenly host's "Regina Coeli"—but as the bride, made new in the flush of youth. One is tempted to think the handmaid who kindled the flame is none other than Circe, who taught Odysseus the glories of passion. It is Penelope who says: "I have eaten the flame."

In Canto xxxix we have seen the four characters who, taken together, give meaning to the man Odysseus, himself absent from the Canto. Even when Circe seems to speak to him, she directs her words to Eurilochus, who is presented as an alternative to the complete man who can be reborn if he attains the humility toward which Circe and Tiresias are ready to guide him; the man who will return from war to peace and to the perfect union with

Penelope. The Canto is like a Chinese ideogram: all the components of Odysseus are set forth, and taken together they produce Odysseus.

To lay the groundwork for this drawing together of threads which mark a path through *The Cantos,* one can point to earlier signposts. The following are only a few of those that recur again and again.

After the stage is set with Odysseus-Pound's journey and the metamorphosis of Acoetes' crew (Cantos i–ii), we find in Canto iv:

> Palace in smoky light,
> Troy but a heap of smouldering boundary stones

The Canto recounts the travels of Odysseus [2] the wily one after he brought about the destruction of Priam's city, for it was he, acting his Eurilochean role as the "man of wide snares," who invented the Wooden Horse ruse. And Pound finds himself leaving behind a wrecked modern civilization to find his way home.

The prime cause of Troy's fall was Helen, who kindled Paris' passion. The wave which "runs into the beach grove," the sea of time floating bits of history onto the shore, tells the poet:

> "Eleanor, ἑλέναυς and ἑλέπτολις!"   (Canto ii)
> Ελέναυς, ἕλανδρος, ἑλέπτολις   (Canto vii)

But Helen, the cause of destruction who winds through the early Cantos, has another aspect. In Canto xx she (woman) is "jungle, /

---

[2] Odysseus is the man who "saw many cities of men, and learnt their minds":
  many men's mannirs   videt et urbes   πολύμητις
  ce rusé personnage, Otis   (Canto lxxviii)

basis of renewal, renewals;" out of which, under the artist's hand, leaps the new born. In Canto XXVII a fragment from a ballata by Guido Cavalcanti shows Helen's creative role, which flowers forth in Canto XXXIX:

> Formando di disio nuova persona
>
> (Canto XXVII)

In Canto XXIX, woman is described:

> Wein, Weib, TAN AOIDAN
> Chiefest of these the second, the female
> Is an element, the female
> Is a chaos
> An octopus
> A biological process
>   and we seek to fulfill . . .

And in Canto XXX, we find woman is by no means evil: "Time is the evil. Evil." Time is the sea which metamorphoses and sends perfection—"the magic moment"—into decay. Thus in Canto XXX again, Artemis complains, "none may seek purity/ Having for foulnesse pity"

> Nothing is now clean slayne
> But rotteth away.

And the same is true of the goddess of love, Aphrodite, who "hath pity on a doddering fool,"

> She tendeth his fyre,
> She keepeth his embers warm.

Canto xxxvi prepares for Canto xxxix with its delineation of woman as natural adjunct to the male, providing "Venter venustus" to his flame. In Canto xxxvi Pound has translated Cavalcanti's "Donna mi prega" canzone, as authority as to what thing is love. "Donna mi prega" prepares for the excursion into the *Odyssey* to portray Odysseus as the man of many devices who finds that his craftiness and resourcefulness cannot, alone, get him home to Ithaca. He needs reverence, and a knowledge of the limitations of man. After "Donna mi prega" comes the bridge to Canto xxxix:

Sacrum, sacrum, inluminatio coitu

With this preparation, the light shines full on Odysseus as the central character of Canto xxxix. The absence of perfection of the Odysseus who fought at Troy is shown as the alternate extremes: passive Elpenor and aggressive Eurilochus. It is only when he has swallowed the essence of Elpenor that Odysseus is prepared to rule in peace at Ithaca. For till then he has been Eurilochus.

If we can accept the myth of Odysseus as the central theme of *The Cantos,* and if we can say that the experience of Odysseus is paralleled by that of Ezra Pound himself, then we shall find that *The Cantos* is not a confused mass of learning, but rather that, like "the rose in the steel dust," the Odysseus myth orders the experience Pound undergoes as he travels through the Land of the Dead and comes forth a different man.

The structure of *The Cantos* is what the narrator sees, as Odysseus before him saw, in Hades. The experience is not Dante's, for Dante began in the *selva oscura* and progressed from the depths of despair to the perfection of the divine world. Pound and Odysseus undergo different experiences. To gain specific ends they withdraw from the everyday world to establish contact with those who have preceded them, so that they can better cope with this world when they return.

Odysseus' purpose is to return home to Ithaca, to Penelope and his son. To do so, he must understand and purify himself after the war at Troy and the affront to Poseidon. Pound's goal is set toward discovering what he is and what his world is. His return home is really his discovery of what his goal as a man is, and home is a settling into some surroundings. Pound is the wanderer, traveling blindly, groping for an answer to the question, "What am I doing in this world? And what kind of world is it, anyway?" Pound is searching for an ethos, as Dante did not have to search because Dante had the Thomistic world laid out for him. Odysseus-Pound has to search, in the absence of a predetermined ethos, his own way.

From the beginning of *The Cantos* the narrator is Odysseus-Pound hearing the speech of those he meets at the fosse in the Land of the Dead. He not only sees men and women in the underworld, but attempts, through metamorphosis, to enter their experiences and understand their spirits. He follows in the wake of an earlier Odysseus; it is to this new Odysseus that Tiresias says in Canto I:

> "A second time? why? man of ill star,
> "Facing the sunless dead and this joyless region? . . ."

The Cantos are the NEKUIA through Canto LI, where Odysseus-Pound reaches the pivot (Ching Ming) and shifts into a history of the world from ancient China, moving to John Adams's America in 1766, and continuing to Adams's death. In Cantos LII–LXXI he considers in action ideas he had found earlier in the poem: those of Confucius and Adams.[3]

The message of Tiresias comes to Odysseus-Pound in Canto XLVII. We have noted that Circe spoke in Canto XXXIX, telling Odysseus he must seek advice from Tiresias before he could return home. We have noted further that Circe spoke in Greek, and was then unintelligible. Now in Canto XLVII the Greek appears translated, signifying that the advice has been digested:

> Who even dead, yet hath his mind entire!
> This sound came in the dark
> First must thou go the road
>
> > to hell
>
> And to the bower of Ceres' daughter Proserpine,
> Through overhanging dark, to see Tiresias,
> Eyeless that was, a shade, that is in hell
> So full of knowing that the beefy men know less than he,
> Ere thou come to thy road's end.

[3] I should like to take this opportunity to thank Myles Slatin of the Department of English of the University of Buffalo for several helpful suggestions. Chief of these is his point that the Chinese and John Adams Cantos may be part of the advice of Tiresias, or rather Tiresias' advice followed by the Odysseus-wanderer. These Cantos would correspond with Tiresias' instructions to Odysseus about how he should placate Poseidon after he had reached Ithaca (*Odyssey* XI. 119 ff.). Tiresias tells Odysseus he must take an oar and wander until he comes to a land where men know not the sea, nor ships, nor mix salt with their food. When a wayfarer should meet Odysseus and tell him the oar is a winnowing fan, then Odysseus should plant the oar, and sacrifice to the sea-god. Thereafter, Odysseus would die in peace. The correspondence is provocative. It suggests that Pound, speaking as a European man, wanders through a history of the world as enacted in far-off lands, where the ideas of Confucius and John Adams mark the way.

> Knowledge the shade of a shade,
> Yet must thou sail after knowledge
> Knowing less than drugged beasts. *phtheggometha*
> *thasson*
> φθεγγώμεθα θᾶσσον

The Greek words re-echo Canto xxxix, where the men first hear
Circe singing, and cry: "Let us call to her quickly!"

Tiresias' advice, which follows, expresses an ethos for individual
man, related to the hell-traveler Odysseus-Pound as he had related
prophecy to Odysseus. Tiresias' advice sums up the drama of Canto
xxxix, where opposites were posed and Circe shown as the catalyst
which resolved the paradox. Speaking of Odysseus' return home
to Penelope, Tiresias says:

> To the cave art thou called, Odysseus,
> By Molü hast thou respite for a little,
> By Molü art thou freed from the one bed
> > that thou may'st return to another

There follows a ritual passage from Hesiod's *Works and Days,*
foretelling "the process" which dominates the Pisan Cantos:

> Begin thy plowing
> When the Pleiades go down to their rest,
>
> > . . . .
>
> When the cranes fly high
> > think of plowing.

This advice, however, is for the moment lost on Ezra Pound. For
though he has succeeded in learning the minds of the shades he

finds in Hades, he has not yet undergone Odysseus' immediate
personal suffering. He understands the ethos Tiresias outlines,
but he is not yet ready to put it into action. Pound has not gained
the reverence and intimate communion Odysseus established with
gods and men after his NEKUIA. One recalls the forbearance Odysseus showed in threading Scylla and Charybdis; his consent to
Circe's instruction to allow himself to be tied to the mast while he
listened to the song of the Sirens; his giving away to Eurilochus'
demand that they put in at Thrinacia; his patience and endurance
in preparing for the ritualistic murder of the suitors who were be-
fouling his home. And even more significant: his deference to
the unburied Elpenor and the crescendo of his reunion with Penelope.

The Pisan Cantos mark that intense personal suffering as the
real world thrusts itself onto Pound. No more is he a traveler in
the Land of the Dead, hearing ancient stories. The social world
as he knew it has been destroyed, and he is confined in his own
home (Italy) by hostile men, as the suitors held Odysseus. Out of
this confrontation with stark fact, Pound comes forth in humility.

Pound is in the prison camp, but in his imagination he is ΟΥ̓
ΤΙΣ—no man—or Odysseus afloat on the sea of time. As ΟΥ̓ ΤΙΣ
he is also Everyman, and ἄχρονος (freed of "time, the evil" Canto
LXXX). As the Pisan Cantos open on destruction, he calls as he
called to Polyphemus, revealing himself to the vengeance of Poseidon: "ΟΥ̓ ΤΙΣ, ΟΥ̓ ΤΙΣ? Odysseus/the name of my family"
(Canto LXXIV).

The explosion of that overweening pride (which Odysseus-
Pound has certainly been guilty of earlier in *The Cantos*) comes as

Pound moves away from Eurilochus and becomes Elpenor, lying with the crew in Circe's swinesty:

> ac ego in harum
> so lay men in Circe's swine-sty;
> ivi in harum ego ac vidi cadaveres animae
>
> (Canto LXXIV)

The Elpenor identification continues through the Pisan Cantos, as Pound calls himself "a man on whom the sun has gone down" and, as he had called Elpenor in Canto I, "a man of no fortune and with a name to come."

The Pisan Cantos revolve around Pound's memory as he lies in the physical swinesty. Memory orders the bits of reminiscence of what he saw in hell and of the companions he fought with— through his life as Ezra Pound, and at Troy as Odysseus. Pound recalls

> Lordly men are to earth o'ergiven
> these the companions   (Canto LXXIV)

as he remembers the companions of his literary existence. We note correspondingly Odysseus' encounter with Agammemnon and Achilles in Hades.

Pound recalls the past as his imagination floats in "periplum," [4] as Odysseus floated from Ogygia and the goddess Calypso to

---

[4] In Canto LIX Pound defines "periplum," after having described that made by Hanno the Carthaginian in Canto XLV:

> Periplum, not as land looks on a map
> but as a sea bord seen by men sailing.

This type of voyage—"see it for yourself"—is the kind Odysseus made, and the kind the time-traveler Odysseus-Pound makes.

Phaeacia, the last stop on his way home. His body rests in the
Pisan camp, where his eyes receive comfort from the landscape and
the soothing winds cool him.[5]

> By no means an orderly Dantescan rising
> but as the winds veer
>
> .   .   .   .
>
>> as the winds veer and the raft is driven
>> and the voices   , Tiro, Alcmene
>> with you is Europa nec casta Pasiphaë
>>   Eurus, Apeliota as the winds veer in periplum

He lies calm, in tune with "the process":

>> How soft the wind under Taishan
>> where the sea is remembered

Taishan is the sacred mountain of the oriental sages, where they
withdraw to breathe "the process." And there may be a hint here
of the final oblation Odysseus makes as he rests in the land where
the oar is thought to be a winnowing fan.

The music of Circe (KALON AOIDIAEI) and of the Virgin ("Regina
Coeli") are transformed in the Pisan Cantos into "La Canzone de li
Uccelli" in Canto LXXV. And in Canto LXXXII music becomes part
of "the process" as Pound sees birds writing notes on the wires:

---

[5] Pound at Pisa may also be thought of as lying in the hut of Eumaeus the swine-
herd, the first person Odysseus spoke to when he returned to Ithaca. Thus the eyes
that enter his tent find their correspondence in those of Athena appearing to Odysseus, and the question Pound asks "sorella della pastorella dei suini" (Canto
LXXXIV), is the one Odysseus asked Eumaeus about the suitors who sat at the absent
Odysseus' table.

three solemn half notes
                    their white downy chests black-rimmed
on the middle wire
                    periplum

Pound's own personal despair weaves through his consciousness:

dry friable earth going from dust to more dust
    grass worn from its root-hold
    is it blacker? was it blacker? Νύξ animae?
    is there a blacker or was it merely San Juan with a belly
                                                    ache
                writing ad posteros
    in short shall we look for a deeper or is this the bottom?
                                        (Canto LXXIV)

Pound's suffering brings home to him the wisdom of Tiresias'
advice:

                    J'ai eu pitié des autres
        probablement pas assez, and at moments that suited my
                                        own convenience

                        .   .   .   .
        Came Eurus as comforter
        and at sunset la pastorella dei suini
                driving the pigs home, benecomata dea
                                        (Canto LXXVI)

Here the Pisan landscape blends with Circe, as she appears in her
role as "comforter," a part of "the process" as is Eurus, the south-
east wind.

Love is stressed throughout by references to Cavalcanti's "Donna mi prega," particularly love's association with memory, "dove sta memoria" (Canto LXXVI). Love is brought full force by "Amo ergo sum" (Canto LXXX), and love is the maintainer of the "magic moment," preventing the slip into metamorphosis and decay:

> What thou lovest well remains,
>   the rest is dross
>   (Canto LXXXI)

Penelope, to Pound, suggests the earth and is referred to in the Pisan Cantos as GEA TERRA, Tellus, Demeter:

> man, earth   :   two halves of the tally
> but I will come out of this knowing no one
> neither they me
>   connubium terrae ἔφατα πόσις ἐμός
>   ΧΘΟΝΙΟΣ, mysterium
>   (Canto LXXXII)

Finally the journey on the raft ends, with a resume of Odysseus:

> the folly of attacking that island
>   and of the force ὑπέρ μόρου
>
> with a mind like that he is one of us
>   Favonus, vento benigno
>   Je suis au bout de mes forces/
>   .   .   .   .
> hast'ou swum in a sea of air strip
>   through an aeon of nothingness,
> when the raft broke and the waters went over me

Prayer follows, and then humility:

> Les larmes que j'ai creées m'inondent
> Tard, très tard je t'ai connue, la Tristesse,
> I have been hard as youth sixty years   (Canto LXXX)

At last Odysseus-Pound has learned, devoured, and digested the wisdom Tiresias spoke in Canto XLVII. In one of the most beautiful passages in *The Cantos* he repeats the core of the blind seer's soothsay, revealed to him as he sits in his tent in the prison camp.

The revelation begins when the famous women appear to Pound in his imagination. They appear to him personally, not as the dead, but they seem to enter his tent "in the timeless air"

> . . . nor is this yet *atasal* [6]
> nor are here souls, nec personae
> neither here in hypostasis, this land is of Dione
> (Canto LXXVI)

The women and the goddesses, wound into the Pisan landscape with the sun, moon, animals, birds, insects, and winds, form a background of permanence and beauty as the Pisan Cantos unfold. With nature, the women form "the process." Then in Canto LXXXI they reveal to Pound the burden of Tiresias' advice:

> Ed ascoltando al leggier mormorio
> there came new subtlety of eyes into my tent,
> whether of spirit or hypostasis,

> . . . .

[6] According to Pound, *"atasal"* means union with god, and comes from Avicenna, the Mohammedan physician and philosopher through whose works Aristotle became known in Europe.

> careless or unaware it had not the
>   whole tent's room
> nor was place for the full Εἰδὼς [7]
> interpass, penetrate
>   casting but shade beyond the other lights
>   sky's clear
>   night's sea
>   green of the mountain pool
>   shone from the unmasked eyes in half-mask's space.
>   What thou lovest well remains

The hymn breaks forth, echoing the words of Canto xLvii: "Pull down thy vanity," "Learn of the green world," "Master thyself, then others shall thee beare."

The hymn leads to the calm stillness of Pound's response:

> But to have done instead of not doing
>   this is not vanity
> To have, with decency, knocked
> That a Blunt should open
>   To have gathered from the air a live tradition
> or from a fine old eye the unconquered flame
> This is not vanity.
>   Here error is all in the not done,
>   all in the diffidence that faltered

Here is the true Odyssean experience breaking through into revelation. The hardness has been metamorphosed by revelation born of knowledge and suffering. And Pound can answer the question posed in the hymnal response of Tiresias' words:

[7] "Εἰδὼς" is the full knowing, or revelation, which occurs later.

> Whose world, or mine or theirs
>> or is it of none?

In the next to the last of the Pisan Cantos, the poet attains *atasal,* or union with the gods whose eyes had entered his tent and revealed to him what he, a man, was. The Canto opens with the resolution of the feud with Poseidon, who becomes part of "the process":

> ὕδωρ
> HUDOR et Pax
>
>   . . . .
>
>> the sage
> delighteth in water
>> the humane man has amity with the hills

Then comes the revelation, as the poet unites with "the process":

> A fat moon rises lop-sided over the mountain
> The eyes, this time my world,
>> But pass and look *from* mine
>>> between my lids
>>>> sea, sky, and pool
>>>> alternate
>>>> pool, sky, sea

And the denouement, the calm after the dark night of the soul has passed, is expressed in the final lines of the last Pisan Canto:

> If the hoar frost grip thy tent
> Thou wilt give thanks when night is spent.